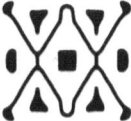

A SIMILITUDE OF NATURE

Giorgio Anselmi on the Images
of the Eighth Celestial Sphere

A Similitude OF NATURE

Giorgio Anselmi *on the* Images
OF THE
EIGHTH CELESTIAL SPHERE

An Edition and Translation of Material
from the *Divinum Opus de Magia Disciplina*

by

Brian Johnson

REVELORE PRESS
Olympia, WA
2025

A Similitude of Nature
GIORGIO ANSELMI ON THE IMAGES OF
THE EIGHTH CELESTIAL SPHERE
An Edition and Translation of Material from the
Divinum Opus de Magia Disciplina

Copyright © 2025 Brian Johnson

First edition published in 2025 by
Revelore Press

All rights reserved. No part of this publication may be reproduced or transmitted in any form or by any means, electronic or mechanical, including photocopy, without permission in writing from the publisher. Reviewers may quote brief passages, as may scholars writing astrological journal articles.

Book and cover design by Joseph Uccello
Cover image: Bavarian manuscript, 15th c. Now Edinburgh, Royal Observatory Crawford Collection, Cr4.6. Used with permission.

PUBLISHER'S CATALOGING-IN-PUBLICATION
(PROVIDED BY CASSIDY CATALOGUING SERVICES, INC.)

Names:	Johnson, Brian, 1985–, author, editor, translator. | Anselmi, Giorgio (Astrologer). Divinum opus de magia disciplina. Selections. English.
Title:	A similitude of nature : Giorgio Anselmi on the images of the eighth celestial sphere: an edition and translation of material from the Divinum opus de magia disciplina / by Brian Johnson.
Description:	First edition. | Olympia, WA: Revelore Press, 2025. | Includes bibliographical references.
Identifiers:	ISBN: 9781947544659 (paperback)
Subjects:	LCSH: Astrology—Early works to 1800. | Stars—Early works to 1800. | Idols and images—Early works to 1800. | Constellations—Early works to 1800. | Zodiac—Early works to 1800. | Magic—Early works to 1800.
Classification:	LCC: BF1724.3 .J64 2025 | DDC: 133.509—dc23

ISBN: 9781947544659

Printed worldwide through Ingram.
Revelore Press
1910 4th Ave E PMB141
Olympia WA 98506
United States

www.revelore.press

ACKNOWLEDGEMENTS

My most humble gratitude belongs first of all to Eric Purdue, whose knowledge of traditional astrological principles, to say nothing of his facility with the Latin language, helped me to cut through a number of semantic knots in the interpretation of this text. Thanks likewise go to Jenn Zahrt for sharing a breadth and depth of astrological expertise far surpassing my own, as well as her infectious enthusiasm for exploring the esoteric techniques employed by obscure historical practitioners of the celestial art.

Contents

Introduction   11

I.
TRACTATE FOUR
On the Methods of Characters, and Examples Thereof.   25

CHAPTER ONE: A Note on the Methods which Are to Be Observed in the Composition of Images.   25

CHAPTER TWO: In What Materials Images and the Like Are to Be Imprinted.   35

CHAPTER FIVE: The Manners of Images Found in Certain Gemstones, and Their Powers.   39

II.
The Fourth Part of the FOURTH TRACTATE of George of Parma, on the Specific Methods Pertaining to the Images of the Eighth Sphere, and on the Methods of their Composition, by Means of Examples.   53

CHAPTER ONE: On the Images which Are Made According to the Twelve Signs of the Zodiac.   55

The image of Aries   59
The image of Taurus   65
The image of Gemini   69
The image of Cancer   73
The image of Leo   77
The image of Virgo   85
The image of Libra   89
The image of Scorpio   93
The image of Sagittarius   99

The image of Capricorn	103
The image of Aquarius	107
The image of Pisces	109

CHAPTER TWO: A Note on the Methods of Composing the
Images of the Eighth Sphere That Lie North of the Zodiac. ... 113

1. Ursa Major	121
2. Ursa Minor	123
3. Draco	123
4. Cepheus	125
5. Boötes	127
6. Corona Borealis	127
7. *al-Rāqeṣ*	129
8. Lyra	129
9. Cassiopeia	131
10. Caput Algol	133
11. Auriga	133
12. Ophiuchus	137
13. Sagitta	137
14. Aquila	139
15. (Cygnus)	141
16. Delphinus	141
17. Equuleus and Pegasus	143
18. Andromeda	145
19. Triangulum	145

CHAPTER THREE: A Note on the Methods Pertaining to Those
Images Made Under the Stars of Those Figures Which
Occupy the Region South of the Zodiac. ... 147

1. Cetus	147
2. Orion	149
3. Eridanus	151
4. Lepus	151
5. Canis Major	153
6. Canis Minor	155
7. Hydra	155
8. Corvus	157
9. Argo Navis	159

10. Centaurus	159
11. Lupus	161
12. (Ara)	163
13. Corona Australis	165

CHAPTER FOUR: On the Methods of Composing Images which Are Not Stellar, but Accompany the Twelve Signs. ... 167

- ¶ to cure cholera, and pains of the stomach, and to preserve one from these ... 167
- ¶ to prevent a bandit from entering a house ... 169
- ¶ so that fire should not ignite in a house ... 171
- ¶ so that neither serpents nor reptiles shall obstruct a place, but flee and die ... 173
- ¶ to make demons disturb, agitate, harass, and vex ... 175
- ¶ to gather together, and multiply, and make fortunate goats, and sheep, and creatures of this sort ... 177
- ¶ so that enemies neither can nor dare to enter a city or place, either by force or deception ... 179
- ¶ to render all locks ready to be opened ... 181
- ¶ so that a dog will not come toward nor bark at a person ... 181
- ¶ so that a horse is halted, (so as) not to pass through where the image is sculpted ... 183
- ¶ so that no animal shall be made to halt, but rather will flee a place as though struck by a whip ... 183
- ¶ so that every ass...shall halt, and, relieved of its burden, bray ... 185
- ¶ to cause all the cattle and bulls...to stop and bellow ... 185
- ¶ so that beasts congregate ... 187
- ¶ so that birds to congregate in the place where it is kept, especially ravens ... 187
- ¶ so that domestic birds and hens congregate in some place and sing ... 189
- ¶ to catch a multitude of fish ... 189

¶ to make fish flee from a lake or river	189
¶ to prevent a field from being cultivated	191
¶ so that goods shall not be sold, either by weight or by quantity	191
¶ so that, cast into the water of a spring or flowing cistern, the waters [halt and…] dry up completely	191
¶ so that all instruments may be bound, and destroyed, and broken	193
¶ so that worms shall gnaw the roots growing in the soil, and whatsoever is fit to be gnawed	195
¶ so that a bow or ballista will not shoot, or otherwise will break	195
¶ for inciting [people] to anger, and making them recalcitrant	197
¶ so that people will cry out and raise their hands	197
¶ so that people will sing	199
¶ so that people will place their clothes on the ground and lie upon them	199
¶ so that women will sing, and comb and scratch their heads	201
¶ so that the inhabitants [of a house or inn] shall not stop eating, nor can they be satisfied	201
¶ so that women will sing	203
¶ so that a woman will go and return to the same place repeatedly	203
Bibliography	204
Colophon	207

INTRODUCTION

THE early decades of the fifteenth century found the practice of astrological image magic in something of a transitional phase within Latin Christendom. Thanks in part to Arabic philosophical and magical works which had begun arriving in the twelfth century, and the charitably broad-minded reception thereof by scholars such as Adelard of Bath, William of Auvergne, and others,[1] the practical science of stellar influences had long since been liberated from the unequivocal judgment—if not the lingering suspicion—that it was merely a mask of propriety under which demons might manipulate the naïve. By the end of the Middle Ages, the prescription of talismans crafted according to the observation of propitious astrological conditions was recognized as a valid form of medical intervention, suitable for no less a patient than the pope himself.[2]

But if astrological images were, in principle, licit, the criteria circumscribing what was permissible in their construction, as well as the learned understanding of by precisely what means they operated, remained in flux. It was not (quite) yet time for Marsilio Ficino's *De vita libri tres*, with its Platonically-informed theory of a cosmic *spiritus* susceptible to attraction by appropriately prepared materials and harmonious musics,[3] to say nothing of an astrological optics like that espoused later still by John Dee in his *Propaedeumata aphoristica*.[4] There was, however, another such doctor-astrologer who was prepared to step into this atmosphere of intellectual ferment in order to promulgate his own synthetic methodology for composing images, one in which "only the present disposition of the heavens is considered"—but the role of mediating intelligences remains as opaque as ever.

---

1 See Klaassen, 2013: 23–6. On the translation of texts from Islamicate Spain, a primary vector for the transmission of these sources, see Burnett, 1992.
2 Weill-Parot, 2019: 256.
3 See Walker, 2000: 12–14 and infra, for a synopsis.
4 See Shumaker, ed. and trans., 1978.

Introduction
Giorgius Parmensis

¶ Born in the city of Parma, at that time part of the Duchy of Milan, presumably not many years before the death of his father in 1386, Giorgio Anselmi was a student and theoretician of the natural sciences, music, and—insofar as can be judged from one of his scant few surviving works, the *Divinum opus de magia disciplina*— magic, of both the natural and demonic varieties. He studied the arts and medicine at Pavia, and was admitted to the faculty of the University of Parma upon its reestablishment in 1412.[5] He was involved in reforming the statutes of the college of physicians there in 1440, and the last we hear of him—short of a somewhat disparaging assessment by Agrippa half a century later[6]—is in the year 1448/9, teaching practical medicine at the University of Bologna.[7] In the intervening years he wrote at least three treatises: an *Astronomia*, preserved in an undated, composite copy,[8] on the nature and motion of the heavenly bodies and their influence upon earthly things; *De musica*, the single extant copy of which is dated 1434,[9] on celestial, instrumental, and vocal music theory; and the *Divinum opus de magia disciplina*.[10] The *Divinum opus*, after a summary definition of magic and its divisions, proceeds to systematically examine several forms of divination, demons and the procedures for conjuring them, magical images which harness the power of their stellar counterparts according to principles of natural similitude, and finally a (seemingly incomplete) discussion of methods for directly influencing living bodies, which gets no farther than *veneficiis*. Like Anselmi's other known works, the *Divinum opus* exists in only one more or less complete manuscript copy, currently held by the Biblioteca Medicea Lau-

---

5 Cox, 2005: 3–4; Thorndike, 1934: 243.
6 Agrippa, in a letter to Trithemius justifying the study of magic and his undertaking to redeem it, writes: "Some writers that I have recently seen promise to speak about magic: Roger Bacon, Robertus Anglicus, Pietro d'Abano, Albertus Magnus, Arnaldus de Villa Nova, Giorgio Anselmi, Picatrix the Spaniard, Cecco d'Ascoli…However, when they do so it is not without certain delusions, unreliable reasoning, or superstitions that are unworthy of anyone who is honest." (Purdue, trans., 2021: 7–8).
7 Cox, 2005: 5; Thorndike, 1934: 243.
8 Vatican City, Biblioteca Apostolica Vaticana, MS Vat. lat. 4080.
9 Milano, Biblioteca Ambrosiana, MS H. 233 inf.
10 Cox, 2005: 5–7.

Introduction

renziana in Florence, Italy.[11] The copyist (and textual integrity) of this manuscript appears to change abruptly between folios 157v and 158r, and it is undated. However, this version of the text is supported by a separate, partial copy at the Biblioteca Apostolica Vaticana, dated 1542 and containing only the fourth part of the fourth tractate,[12] on the images of the eighth celestial sphere, corresponding to folios 196r–224r in the Florence manuscript.

Natural Magic and Celestial Instruments

¶ The general paradigm within which Anselmi's exposition of astral images unfolds is the Ptolemaic-Aristotelian scholasticism of his university curriculum. The changeable things of the sublunary elemental world are subject to movement by prior efficient causes—general ones affecting generic classes of things, or the condition of things in general across spans of time and space, particular ones predicating particular individual cases—and those causes include extraterrestrial bodies like the Sun, Moon, planets, and stars.[13] It is precisely in terms of general causes and effects that Anselmi explains the operation of his own images, based as they are upon that outermost and hence most general of celestial causes (short of the *primum mobile* and empyrean), the sphere of the fixed stars.[14]

Thus, by virtue of their inherent powers and motions, the perfect, impassible heavens work in a basically mechanistic way upon earthly things of corresponding natures;[15] a gemstone, for instance, carefully selected for its Jupiterian qualities and engraved with an appropriate talismanic image, would necessarily move in sympathy with the benefic actuations of the planet Jupiter. The nature of this correspondence or sympathy can be understood

---

11 Florence, Biblioteca Medicea Laurenziana, MS Plut. 44.35.
12 Biblioteca Apostolica Vaticana, MS Vat. lat. 5333.
13 See Aristotle, *Physics* II.3, and Ptolemy, *Tetrabiblos* I.2. For Ptolemy's doctrine especially concerning astrological causes of general phenomena, see *Tetrabiblos* II; on the Medieval reception of certain elements of this doctrine, see Bezza, 2015.
14 Plut. 44.35, 118v.
15 Plut. 44.35, 118r–v, 119v.

INTRODUCTION

in terms of certain occult properties shared by individual substances participating in a specific form which they hold in common, an accepted principle of medical science by the fourteenth century.[16] Indeed, Albert the Great in his book *De mineralibus* had explained the marvelous powers inherent in precious stones as a function of just such specific forms, each of which mediates "between...the heavenly powers by which it is conferred, and the matter of the combination into which it is infused."[17] Anselmi's own conception of such formal similarity between that which is above and that which lies below may have derived, at least partly, from a Platonist belief that all of creation is informed by consonant series of numerical ratios, embodied in the tones produced by heavenly cycles and epicycles no less than in the workings of the human soul, a vision of cosmic harmony he espoused more explicitly in the *De musica*.[18]

The celestial bodies, in themselves, are devoid of manifest elemental qualities, and so those sublunary beings and contingencies to which particular planets or constellations correspond can be known only by inference born of long-observed correlations of motion and activity.[19] Anselmi was an empiricist; commenting upon the "marvelous virtues and abilities" which minerals possess due to their harmony with "the movement and power and nature of the sphere above," he credits human knowledge of such coordinations between the celestial and terrestrial to observant investigation, presided over by "mistress experience."[20] And while he concedes that astrologically elected images may not in fact be able to manifest their powers perpetually or eternally, given the ever-fluctuating state of the heavens, or to do so indifferently for each and every patient, he defends their capacity to retain such "great and famous properties" in principle based

---

16 Weill-Parot, 2019: 256–7.
17 Albertus, *Book of Minerals* II.i.4; see Wyckoff, trans., 1967: 65.
18 See Tomlinson, 1993: 75–7. This arithmosophic cosmology can be traced directly to Plato's *Timaeus* 35–36b, and likely reflects prior Pythagorean doctrines.
19 Cox, 2005: 23–4. Contrary to Aristotelians like Anselmi (following, for instance, *On the Heavens* I.3, II.7), other traditions espoused various theories concerning the material composition of the heavens; see, e.g., Macrobius, *Commentary on the Dream of Scipio* I.xi.8.
20 Plut. 44.35, 127v.

upon his own observation of experiments to that effect.²¹

This was all fairly uncontroversial in Anselmi's time. Already in the thirteenth century, the *Speculum astronomiae*—an anonymous apologia for astrological studies likely penned by Albert himself²²—had argued that "...if God...has ordered this world in such a manner, that He...should wish to operate through the created things found in these four inferior elements, using the mute and deaf stars as if they were instruments...what could be more desirable to a thinking man than to have a middle science which might teach us how this and that change in the mundane world is effected by the changes in the celestial bodies?"²³

This cosmology was not a strictly materialist one, however. Aristotle attributed to the celestial spheres a principle of motion not essentially different from his first principle, the immaterial unmoved mover,²⁴ and elsewhere he described them in terms which could be construed as imputing a soul (ἔμψυχος).²⁵ Later interpretations differed as to whether this "soul" were rational or merely a principle of motion, but by the end of the thirteenth century the understanding espoused by authorities including Thomas Aquinas and Albert was that the movers of the heavenly spheres were indeed rational, though even these doctors of the church remained ambivalent as to whether they could properly be called angels.²⁶

But if there were even potentially room for angels in the chain of astral-terrestrial causality, there was certainly room for demons. Albert accepted the proposition that demons could manipulate or appropriate the influences of celestial bodies for their own ends, though they themselves remained bound beneath the heavens,²⁷ and Michael Scot went so far as to suggest that at least some of the constellations' influence in the sublunary world was ultimately demonic in origin.²⁸ Anselmi, for his part, while attributing the generation and corruption of changeable elemental

---

21 Plut. 44.35, 129r–v.
22 See Zambelli, 1992: 54–9.
23 Burnett et al., trans., 1992: 221.
24 Wolfson, 1962: 67; see Aristotle, *Metaphysics* XII.8.
25 Wolfson, 1962: 68; see Aristotle, *On the Heavens* II.2.
26 Wolfson, 1962: 87–9; Zambelli, 1992: 92–4.
27 Page, 2019: 236.
28 Page, 2019: 241.

INTRODUCTION

bodies to their natural inclination to follow the movements of the heavens according to principles of likeness,[29] in some places implies that angels, or perhaps demons, are in fact the proximate movers of those sublunary things, albeit in accordance with the guiding forms embodied by the stars.[30] Indeed, the precise mechanism by which Anselmi understood the motive force of the stars to find its way to the realm of elemental bodies remains rather vague in the *Divinum opus*. We find no explicit reference to the theory of multiplication of species, *à la* Roger Bacon, or to the rays of al-Kindi, though either or both could easily have been tacitly assumed in a scientific text of the fifteenth century, and nothing in the *opus* seems to preclude them as explanations. The most that Anselmi leaves us with is a brief allusion to the operation of magnets by way of a general analogy to sympathetic action at a distance; still, for one so musically-minded, perhaps it was after all simply a matter of vibrations, like resonance in the harmonically tuned strings of a lute.

Another ambiguity lies in his use of both tropical and sidereal frames of reference. On one hand, Anselmi clearly distinguishes between the Zodiac *signs* and their corresponding *constellations*. He locates particular stars of the latter in terms of their place beneath a given degree of the tropical ecliptic,[31] itself divided into the traditional houses,[32] and even makes reference to the historically observable phenomenon of precession.[33] At times, however, his terminology appears ambivalent, as though he has not fully harmonized the language of some older sources which did not recognize such a distinction; reference is made to the luminaries moving under a zodiacal *image* (Anselmi's usual term for a constellation) in one place, under a *sign* in another,[34] for instance. Granted, it is the influence of the constellations—the stars themselves—with which Anselmi is primarily concerned here. For while he allows that "each one of the signs of the Zodiac

---

29 Plut. 44.35, 1r, 121v.
30 Plut. 44.35, 47r–v: "...those directed by the nature and quality of the fixed stars to move those things and contingencies which the stars themselves govern...".
31 See, e.g., Vat. lat. 5333, 10r.
32 E.g., Vat. lat. 5333, 21r.
33 Vat. lat. 5333, 26r–v.
34 Compare, e.g., Vat. lat. 5333, 1v and 10v.

Introduction

governs the things of this world below," so too do "the remaining images" which "accompany the twelve signs of the Zodiac," in the same way as "the remaining stellar images, thirty-six in number, which are depicted outside the Zodiac."[35]

In both his theoretical perspective and the specific examples he formulates, Anselmi seems to present a novel, and not always fully articulated, synthesis of various sources and explanations for the mechanics of magic. Not only in his juxtaposing of chapters on exorcistic ceremonies with those pertaining to a more naturalistic sort of image magic, but within the discourse of those respective subdivisions themselves, Anselmi neither entirely distinguishes "natural" from "demonic" magic, nor consistently represents the role of spiritual agents—or other bodiless entities, like the heavenly signs—in the processes of nature, including the operation of magical images. Yet, if nothing else, Anselmi appears to have maintained a relatively unvarying cosmological viewpoint throughout his oeuvre, as the secondary causal role he imputes to spirits in the *Divinum opus* is precisely what we find in his *Astronomia* as well.[36]

Parallels and Precedents, or the Lack Thereof

¶ Anselmi's treatment of magical images, with which the present volume is primarily concerned, appears to be largely in agreement with, if not directly informed by, the philosophical authorities of his age, and no less uncomfortably poised between licit natural science and the forbidden invocation of demons. The eleventh chapter of Albert's *Speculum* is devoted to his own attempt at drawing just such a distinction, and comes down in favor of a method for constructing purely "...astronomical images, which eliminates the filth, does not have suffumigations or invocations and does not allow exorcisms or the inscription of char-

---

35 Vat. lat. 5333, 1r.
36 Cox, 2005: 25.

acters, but obtains [its] virtue solely from the celestial figure..."[37] Albert attributes his explanation for the efficacy of such images to the ninth sentence of (pseudo-)Ptolemy's *Centiloquium*,[38] and Caroti *et al.* have demonstrated that the worked example of an image which Albert provides likely bears a direct debt to the *De imaginibus* of Thabit ibn Qurra.[39] Albert's discrimination of exorcistic from strictly celestial talismans, while drawing distinctions which cut across those categories quite differently from the ones Anselmi adumbrates, certainly provided a model for later taxonomies, including the *Parmense*'s own delineation of the "ceremonial" and "natural" methods of composing images,[40] although Anselmi withholds the explicit moral judgment which is rather the entire point of Albert's treatise.

A chronological intermediary between the *Speculum* and the *Divinum opus*—and perhaps a direct source for Anselmi's articulation of an image magic which might be either astrological, demonic, or a bit of both—is the *De occultis et manifestis* of Antonio da Montolmo. Antonio lectured on grammar, medicine, and astrology at the University of Bologna nearly a century prior to the time that Anselmi was teaching there, but it is not implausible that the latter could have encountered a copy of his treatise still in circulation amongst the faculty. The fourth chapter of Antonio's work exactly predicts Anselmi's in the three methodologies it posits for empowering talismanic objects, as well as in the observation that such workings are most effective when a conducive ordering of the heavens is combined with aid from spiritual assistants persuaded by words and suffumigations.[41]

Nonetheless, where Anselmi's instructions do recommend any sort of verbal utterance on the part of the artificer, this is always of a purely optative nature, "so that the power of the artificer may fall upon" the work,[42] never an imperative that might potentially be

---

37 Burnett et al., trans., 1992: 247.
38 Burnett et al., trans., 1992: 271. Namely: "In generation and corruption earthly forms are subordinate to the celestials; wherefore they that frame images, do then make use of them, by observing when the planets do enter into those constellations or forms." (Houlding, ed., 2006, https://www.skyscript.co.uk/centiloquium1.html).
39 Zambelli, 1992: 296-7.
40 Plut. 44.35, 118v-119r.
41 See Weill-Parot, 2012.
42 Plut. 44.35, 119r. For examples of such prescribed speech, see "Chapter Four:

construed as addressing another rational being—with the possible exception of one image which is crafted for the explicit purpose of calling upon a demon to harass a victim.[43] In any case, the *Divinum opus* demonstrates that by the early fifteenth century, at least some practitioners were reflecting upon, if not thoroughly embracing, the *Speculum*'s program for a sanitized astral magic.

While in some cases Anselmi's sources for the *Divinum opus* can be identified with a fair degree of confidence,[44] in others, such as the astral images of the fourth tractate, things are less certain. The *De imaginibus* of Thabit can only be compared to Anselmi's work in general terms.[45] Thabit's selection of experiments is more limited in scope, and rather more open-ended in its instructions, given that each posited image requires a unique election, keyed to the ascendant—whether natal, horary, or generic—of the specific subject or inquiry to which it pertains. Anselmi's images, by contrast, make use of fairly rote celestial arrangements, intended to be capable of influencing whole classes of individual things and circumstances ruled over by various signs and asterisms, though he also addresses such relatively complex techniques as primary direction of the natal chart, considering their implications for determining the proper zodiacal talisman to utilize at a particular time in a patient's life.[46] Again, where the *Divinum opus* prescribes at least broad guidelines for the sort of materials in which it would be most apt to craft a given image, namely those corresponding in their nature to the desired qualities of the primary celestial body dictating the hour of its election[47]—most often the Sun or Moon in Anselmi's examples—*De imaginibus* is seemingly indifferent to the question of material basis, stating more than once that the artificer should simply

---

On the Methods of Composing Images Which Are Not Stellar, But Accompany the Twelve Signs". This again recalls the theory expounded in al-Kindi's *De radiis*, e.g. "And among all forms of speech, the optative has greater efficacy, inasmuch as desire indicates the words' significance and from desire proceeds their natural existence, and therefore their rays effect motion in competent matter greater than other species of rays." (Gosnell, trans., 2022: 67–8).

43 See Vat. lat. 5333, 31r.
44 Burnett, 1996: 66.
45 I have referred to the edition by Carmody, 1960, and that of Bohak and Burnett, 2021.
46 See the examples in "Chapter One: On the Images Which Are Made According to the Twelve Signs of the Zodiac."
47 Plut. 44.35, 120v–121r.

INTRODUCTION

use "whatever [metal] you wish."[48] While Anselmi may indeed have referred to *De imaginibus*, known in its Latin form since the twelfth century,[49] in formulating his practical methodology, Anselmi's images, no less than those of Thabit, are constructed from astrological first principles, and are perhaps of his own derivation.

A text bearing a greater similarity to Anselmi's, at least in its formal structure, is another book "on images," this one first appearing in Latin in book II, chapter 12 of the *Picatrix* where it is attributed to Hermes, and which was copied repeatedly down through the sixteenth century.[50] Anselmi's chapter "On the Images Which Are Made According to the Twelve Signs of the Zodiac" may represent a further evolution of this Hermetic tradition, as both texts are organized around the twelve signs of the Zodiac, their instructions focused upon the proper disposition of the benefics, malefics, Sun, Moon, and Mercury, as well as the proper planetary hours for working; moreover, a number of the images clearly derive from a common source. However, the specific electional prescriptions in the two texts are entirely different, with Hermes giving consideration to the signs' decan divisions, and more negative injunctions as to where or in what condition a given celestial body should *not* be, whereas Anselmi's prescriptions are more direct, stipulating relative aspects and sometimes degrees of exaltation.

One final source which also undoubtedly shares a genealogy with some of the examples given in the *Divinum opus* is the pseudo-Ptolemaic *De imaginibus super facies signorum*. Like the Hermetic text just mentioned, this one too is organized around a sequential progression through the signs, noting in particular the rising decan under which each of its images should be made.[51] The prescribed forms and intended effects of at least some of these images appear to closely correspond to certain of those images which Anselmi says "are not stellar, but accompany the twelve signs,"[52] yet Anselmi (or his proximate source) largely refrains from any discussion of explicit decan placements, and instead

---

48 Bohak and Burnett, eds., 2021: 122, 152.
49 Bohak and Burnett, eds., 2021: 37.
50 Juste, 2023b, https://ptolemaeus.badw.de/work/64.
51 See Bohak and Burnett, eds., 2021: 35–6, 181–9.
52 Vat. lat. 5333, 29r ff.

correlates this selection of talismans to the Moon's co-ascension with various zodiacal and extra-zodiacal stars. While it also entered the Latin milieu through a translation from the Arabic, the *De imaginibus* of pseudo-Ptolemy survives in a significantly greater number of manuscripts than the text credited to Hermes;[53] however, as far as I am aware, Anselmi's apparent reception and reworking of either of these texts has heretofore gone unremarked in the scholarship. Anselmi's familiarity with sources indebted to Arabic astronomical science is further demonstrated by his inclusion of a number of constellation and star names which are clearly Latin calques of the Arabic nomenclature,[54] perhaps deriving from interpolations made in Arabic translations of Ptolemy's Μαθηματικὴ σύνταξις (the *Almagest*), from which the first Latin versions of that text were made.[55]

Translating the Fourth Tractate

¶ The present translation is based upon those parts of the *Divinum opus* especially concerned with astral images and their artificial reproduction, encompassing both practical instructions for their composition and use, and explanations of the principles by which they operate. The first part, largely of a theoretical nature, comes from folios 118r–121r and 127r–130r of Florence, Biblioteca Medicea Laurenziana, MS Plut. 44.35. The remainder, describing the figures, qualities, and powers of images crafted in likeness to (most of) the forty-eight Ptolemaic constellations, as well as a number which are otherwise informed by celestial counterparts, comes primarily from Biblioteca Apostolica Vaticana, MS Vat. lat. 5333, which I have frequently found to provide more accurate

---

53 See Juste, 2023, https://ptolemaeus.badw.de/work/4.
54 See in particular "Chapter Two: A Note on the Methods of Composing the Images of the Eighth Sphere That Lie North of the Zodiac" and "Chapter Three: A Note on the Methods Pertaining to Those Images Made Under the Stars of Those Figures Which Occupy the Region South of the Zodiac".
55 The earliest known Latin translation of the *Almagest* was Gerard of Cremona's, in the latter half of the twelfth century; see Zieme, 2023: 4. Other Arabic works combining Ptolemaic and Arabic star nomenclature, such as the *Ṣuwar al-Kawākib* or "Book of the Fixed Stars" of al-Sufi, were also known to the Latin Renaissance; see Hafez, 2010: 249–251, and Kunitzsch, 1987.

Introduction

readings of that part of the text than the Florence manuscript does, though I have made emendations based upon Plut. 44.35 in some cases. All of this is part of the fourth tractate of the *opus*, "On the Methods of Characters, and Their Examples."

This translation aims to accurately convey to modern English readers the sense of the original text's often very technical discussions of the theory and practice of astrological image magic. Anselmi's style is sometimes quite terse, so occasional editorial insertions for clarity have been made; these are indicated by round brackets ( ). He also uses a variety of Latin and Arabic astrological, mineralogical, and other specialized terminology, some of which more or less closely corresponds to modern usage, some which does not. Deciphering all of this has entailed a certain degree of educated inference, in addition to much outside research, and misinterpretations on the part of the translator are not out of the question. Lingering uncertainties are addressed in the footnotes, and readers are invited to draw their own conclusions from the accompanying transcription of the Latin.

I have adhered to the following conventions in transcribing the manuscript texts:

¶ Curly brackets { } indicate obvious errors present in the manuscripts, retained here for the sake of transparency.

¶ Angle brackets < > indicate editorial insertions to correct obvious unintentional omissions in the manuscripts.

¶ Otherwise, the spelling of commonly used words has been normalized, both within and between manuscripts. Punctuation and capitalization follow the manuscript copies as closely as human transcription realistically allows, without regard to modern usage standards, though proper names have been consistently capitalized.

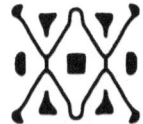

[*from* MS Plut. 44.35]

Divinum Opus de Magia Disciplina

[118r]

Tractatus quartus de modis et exemplis charap-terum[1] Capitulum primum. Notificatio modorum qui servandi sunt in compositione inmaginum.[2]

CHAPTER ONE: A NOTE ON THE METHODS WHICH ARE TO BE OBSERVED IN THE COMPOSITION OF IMAGES.

1

<IN>[3]MAGO EST SIMILITUDO NATURALIS PER ARTIFI-ciosam electionem inducta ad confortandum res naturales et operationes mirabiles: intelligi-mus autem per naturales res eas circa quas sunt philoso-phorum considerationes et asupernaturalibus absolute et sunt quae dependent ex elementum motibus et elementatorum propter actionem et passionem qualitatum contrarialium. Sunt vero generationes et corruptiones, hoc in inferiori orbe consequentes alterationes elementales in vegetabi-libus et plantis et animalibus per pestilentias et fames quae veniunt in regionibus: et morales ope-rationes intelligimus morales artes et exercitia circa quae versantur operationes humane et ani-mantium instinctus: fiunt autem intentiones ima-ginum constituendarum eas quatenus post radi-ces universales aut etiam particulares forent ali-quid fixum et perdurabile superius confortans et eum qualiter in radicibus quotiens bene di-sposite sunt ex praestitis ut sequantur proprii effe-ctus: et est imaginum radicibus idem: fortificantur

---

1 Read: characterum.
2 Read: imaginum.
3 Rubricated initial letters missing in the manuscript.

GIORGIO ANSELMI/*Brian Johnson*

[118r]

TRACTATE FOUR:
*ON THE METHODS OF CHARACTERS,
AND EXAMPLES THEREOF.*

CHAPTER ONE: *A Note on the Methods
Which Are to Be Observed in the Composition of Images.*

An image is a similitude of nature,
induced by artful election to strengthen
natural things, and perform miraculous works.
And we understand by "natural things" those around which
the contemplations of the philosophers revolve, and from which the
 supernatural is absent;
those which are entirely dependent upon movements[4] of the
 elements
and elemental things through the action and
passivity of contrary qualities. Indeed,
generations and corruptions are, here in this lower sphere,
consequent upon elemental alterations in growing things
and plants and animals, due to plagues and
famines which come upon places. And morally accountable works[5]
we understand to be those deliberative arts and occupations
with which works of human and creaturely
instigation are concerned. But the purpose
of constructing images is that, insofar as
the universal, or even particular, roots[6] are relatively
fixed and enduring, that which is superior strengthens (what is
 inferior).
And just as when the roots are well disposed
the proper results follow from what has preceded,
so too with the roots of images:

> 4 *motibus*. Throughout the text, Anselmi's usage of the nouns and verbs denoting motion should be understood in the Aristotelian sense (see the *Physics* III.1), comprising any and all forms of change, qualitative or quantitative; the actualization of a potential.
> 5 *morales operationes*. The contextual sense seems to pertain to willed acts in general.
> 6 *radices*; sg. *radix*. Anselmi primarily seems to use this term in reference to the principal governing signs in a natal or electional chart, though in some cases it appears to imply the chart as a whole. Because of this ambiguity, I have generally opted not to attempt a more precise translation than "root".

Divinum Opus de Magia Disciplina

[118v]

itaque per imaginum compositionem rerum effectus: etenim qualiter aratus diligenter et ster-
coratus ager bone glebae fructificat uberius: sic
per imaginem decenter factam fortificatur radicis opus et prohibetur malum et damnum
quod fortassis sine ipsa posset accidere aut pro
multa et graviori parte obtunditur: Sunt vero
imagines quedam ad res universales et accidentia movenda et sunt quae respiciunt regiones
et sectas et regna et quae sequuntur principes be-
llorum duces et imperatores: Sunt de hinc quae
particulares concernunt res et accidentia, perso-
nas singulares et alias res certas: Sunt autem
quae monstrant vim et posse supra plures res
indestincte et sunt haec quae faciunt ad illarum
similitudinem quae octavo in orbe finguntur
haec siquidem neque hominem habent aut avem vel
canem sed speciem humanam equinam caninas
et huiusmodi reliqua. Sunt quidem componendarum et figurandarum imaginum modi tres:
unus quidem naturalis et est quotiens pro imaginis factura sola celestis praesens dispositio reci-
pitur: Alius econtrario pure ceremonialis, cuius
est modus cum artifex ad compositionem solam

the effects of things are thus strengthened by the composition of images.
For just as a diligently ploughed and manured
field of good soil bears fruit more plentifully, so
by an image properly fashioned the work of the root is strengthened,
and misfortune and injury
that may otherwise befall are prevented, or (at least)
for the greater and more serious part blunted. But
some images are for moving things and accidents[7] in general,
and are those which pertain to regions
and sects and kingdoms, and which are sought by princes,
war leaders, and emperors; hence they are those which
mix together particular things and accidents,
individual persons and other discrete things. And they are
those (images) which demonstrate force and power over many things
indifferently, and these are the ones which people fashion in
similitude of those (figures) which are arranged in the eighth sphere;
for these do not preside over *a* person, or *a* bird, or
a dog,[8] but rather the species that is human, or equine, or canine,
and likewise the rest. There are at least three methods
of composing and forming images.
One, indeed, is natural, and this is when
only the present disposition of the heavens is considered in fashioning an image.
Another, quite to the contrary, is ceremonial,
the method of which has the artificer simply taking material for the composition

---

7 *accidentia.* The sense is that of Aristotelian logic (see *Topica* I.5), contrasting essential (defining) and accidental (qualifying) properties, which Anselmi uses to distinguish "things in themselves" (*res*) from their qualities and circumstances.

8 Emphatic italics added for clarity.

accipit materiam quotiens volet et rem vel figuram imprimendam et cerimonias quasdam
cum orationibus et advocationibus et coniura-
tionibus et huius similibus ad solum locum inten-
dens cum his: Tertius est modus hos duos coniun-
gens: Est vero cum artifex stante celi dispositione
certa et apta dearticulata certa materia figuras
imprimit ad cuiusque rei similitudinem et additur
ceremonias, fumigia, victimas, verba, orationes
advocat praesentes demones et spiritus ut adsi-
stante et proponit easdem his cum eorum nominibus, impressionibus et charapteribus suis et tandem loco disponit: et creditur apud doctos modus
hic fortior: Exequemur autem de uno quoque horum
modorum si deo placuerit: Imprimis quidem de
eorum compositione quam naturalem dicimus
fore, cum videlicet sola orbis attenditur dispositio in compositione et si in hoc sit opus rem nomi-
nare pro qua fit: Quod quidem est uti cadat
supra eam artificis vis: itaque ad earum compositionem diligenter intendum erit, quatenus
dispositio celi sub qua formanda fuerit fortis sit
ut nullo modo stella motrix principalis sit impe-
dita nisi fortassis fuerit imago ad impediendum

GIORGIO ANSELMI / *Brian Johnson*

at whatever time they wish, along with the thing or figure
to be imprinted, and some ceremonies
with orations and invocations and conjurations
and the like, setting out for some solitary place
with these. The third method combines these two:
indeed, it is when the artificer sets a certain and suitable disposition of the heavens,
together with certain materials, imprinting figures
in similitude of each thing, and adding
ceremonies, suffumigations, sacrifices, words, orations,
inviting the presence of demons and spirits as assistants,
and designating these same with their names,
impressions, and characters, and finally
arranging them in some location—and it is believed among the learned that
this method is the more powerful. We, however, will investigate each one of these methods,
if it please God. Firstly, in any case, we concern ourselves with
the composition of those images which we declare to be natural,
namely those in the composition of which only the disposition of the heavenly sphere is attended to,
and if in this work the thing is to be named
for which the work is done, it is merely so that
the power of the artificer may fall upon it. Therefore diligent attention shall be paid to
the composition of the image, insofar as
the disposition of the heavens under which it is fashioned shall be strong,
so that by no means shall the principal motive star be impeded—
unless perhaps an image should be intended to cause hindrance—

mediocriter siquidem disposita aut debili exi-
stente non veniet unusquisque profectus quem optamus.
Sit rursus foelix et praeter fortitudines essentiales
quarum praecipue sunt domicilium et honor et
hayz possideat ab horoscopo locum qui illius
formam et fortunam adaugeat et sit convenientia inter haec omnia ad opus imaginis. Est
vero initium compositionis earum quae res accidentia generalia cernunt ex maioribus radicibus
assummendum: ad quarum vis particulares
res et accidentia satis est fundamentum particu-
laribus ex radicibus habere, sic et earum quae
res et accidentia sperantur. Et nunquam promoveat
artifex ad earum compositionem qui universales res movere habent et accidentia nisi motus
ab his ad quos magnopere spectat illarum gu-
bernatio: spectat autem ad reges et principes quin
fortius moture sunt quas illi manibus suis compo-
nunt: ac saltem compositioni praesens ipse sit apro-
priata verba super eas dicat, quatenus pariter
concurrant supra imaginem voluntas et effectus inferioris et superioris orbis:
sic et quae sin-
gulares ad radices fiunt domini sui mandata for-
mande sunt vel ipse appropriata proferat verba

neither an indifferent disposition nor the presence of a debility
coming to be in any effect which we elect.
Rather, (the star) shall be fortunate, and moreover possess the
 essential dignities—
principal of which are the domicile, and exaltation, and
hayz[9]—from the ascendant, the house which
augments (a native's) form and fortune, and there shall be harmony
among all of these in the crafting of an image. Indeed, it is at
the beginning of the images' composition that those things (and)
 accidents
in general are discerned which are to be received from the major
 roots;
to make particular
things and accidents strong, it suffices to have a foundation in
 particular
roots, and so too for those
things and accidents which are desired. And the artificer shall never
 proceed
to the composition of images which have the capacity
to move things and accidents in general without diligently seeking
 the influence
upon these things of those which govern them.
And why seek after kings and princes when
the influence of those things composed by the artificer's own hands
 is stronger?
In any case, the artificer shall be personally present at the composition of the image,
saying the appropriate words over it, so that
the will and effect of both the
inferior and superior sphere shall be in accord upon the image,
and thus the individual (parts)
come to be shaped (in correspondence) to the roots by the command
 of their master,
or his pronouncement of the proper words.

---

9 A gender- and sect-based planetary dignity.

Divinum Opus de Magia Disciplina

omnis vero imago ita imprimenda est ut patentes
sint omnes eius lineationes et concavationes quatenus
insuis partibus similitudines dicentis existat: Non
equidem vis perdurat imaginis nisi quantum eius
figuratio: Sunt vero qui non omni tempore fundunt
aut figurant sed per partes unicuique illarum eligen-
tes. veruntamen videtur esse proportio compositionis imaginis ad suas partes qualis generationis animalis
et eius reductionis in lucem siquidem conceptio-
nis hora faetus in ventre dat accidentia: eductio-
nis vero vitae in hanc lucem processum: sic et in arte
satis est si eligatur fundamento domus: est vero
omnis imago fortius movens quae impressa fuerit in re cuius est pariter natura similes res
et accidentia movere veluti cum fuerit imago
ad agendas divitias et imprimitur in metallo
Iovis imago aut gemma quae Iovis naturam
sectatur et motum: Et si rursus hic pro quo fit
sit ad id radice sua pronus Iovialis quidem
aut ex conversione annuae radicis: sic si patria vel
regnio fuerit de his quae Iuppiter admovet
vel regulat: ita et imago ad victoriam in bello
sculpeda est inferior, Mars in gemma quae illius
motum sectatur et sit martialis et eductus ex

But every image is thus imprinted so that
all of its lines and curves are manifest in such a way that
the prescribed similitudes are present in its parts;
certainly, the power of an image endures only as long as its
form. Indeed, there are some who do not cast
or shape an image all at once, but by parts, electing each one of
them.
In any case, it is evident that the proportionality
of parts in the composition of an image is like the generation of an
animal
and its birth,[10] since the hour of conception
gives the fetus in the womb its accidents;
indeed the birthing of a living thing is analogous to the way that,
in handicraft, it suffices if the foundation of a house is (well) chosen.
But
every image is more capable of moving that in respect of which it has
been impressed;
it is the nature of similar things
and accidents to move together—just as when an image is fashioned
to generate wealth, and it is imprinted in a metal
of Jupiter, or a gemstone which follows the nature and movement of
Jupiter,
and if, moreover, this is fashioned for one
who is at least inclined to Jupiter by their root,
or by the root according to their annual (solar) return:[11] for instance,
if (their) homeland or
region[12] were conducted or regulated by Jupiter according to (either
of) these.
And in the same way, then, an image of Mars for victory in war
is sculpted in a gemstone which
follows that planet's movement, and is of a martial nature, and has
been extracted from

---

10 *reductionis in lucem*, i.e. literally "being brought into the light".
11 *ex conversione annuae radicis*, i.e. if the chart for their solar return/revolution (for which, see de Vore, 2002: 383; Lewis, 2003: 617–22) favors Jupiter (or possibly natal Jupiter) thusly.
12 Reading *regio* for *regnio*.

loco quem Mars gubernat, sic et in ceteris par inditium.

Capitulum secundum in qua materia imprimuntur imagines et similia.

IMPRESSIONES ET IMAGINES ET CHARAPteres et similes figurationes et proprie quas naturales fore praediximus non cerimoniales comunes sunt cuique materie, verum quotiens in materia fuerit cuius est natura movere opus quasi duplicatur vis imaginis: Est autem materia metallum hoc aut gemma: Notum vero fit ex his quae de rerum proprietatibus scripta sunt habere metalla: sic et gemmas proprietates movendi et nos iam scriptimus in superioribus quarum stellarum sectantur motus: Cuius rei est ex exemplum: intentio est imaginis ad honores laicos: Scimus solem hominum motorem: aurum supra metalla honoratur et sectatur Solis naturam: fit ergo ut impressio in hac fortioris motus existat, sit et in lapillo impressa qui Cabrates nominatus est gemma est christallo similis, cuius est natura se ferentem honorari et naturam Solis sectatur<.> Ita si allectorio lapide fuerit impressa: et qualis est de metallis et lapillis viditium, par etiam plantis

[120v]

a place which Mars governs, and likewise thus for the rest.

Chapter Two: *In What Materials Images and the Like Are to Be Imprinted.*

IMPRESSIONS, AND IMAGES, AND CHARACTERS,
and similar figures, and especially those
that are to be natural, as we have said, not ceremonial,
share common materials, but shall always be in a material
the nature of which is to set in motion the work (in question), so as to
double the power of the image. And this material shall be a metal
or a gemstone; indeed, it has been made known which of these (latter)
have properties that metals are written to possess,
so those same properties will move gemstones as well, and we
have already written of those stars
the movement of which they follow. For example, (consider) an
image that is intended to confer secular honors: we know that the Sun
is what moves people; gold is honored above all metals,
and follows the nature of the Sun; therefore
an impression made in this material shall have a stronger motive force. It may also be
engraved in a stone which is called *cabrates*,[13]
a gemstone similar to crystal, the nature of which is
to advance honors, and which follows the nature of the Sun;
likewise if it should be engraved in an *alectoria* stone.[14] And just as
we see with metals and stones, so too plants

---

13 See Albertus, *Book of Minerals* II.ii.9, "kabrates".
14 A stone extracted from the gizzard of a cock. See Pliny, *Natural History* 37.54; Albertus, *Book of Minerals* II.ii.1.

et herbulis, verum non perdurant haec qualiter mineralia: Non est autem nostrum in praesentia naturas et proprietates mineralium dicere. Quacumque sint in quavis compositione cuius vis imaginis plures numero planete adiutores motus est autem principalis sicut fortior motus, ita adhibenda materia illi concors: Quod si fuerit opus imaginis ad duas aut plures res diversas, sit materia ex coniunctis metallis aut contritis gemmis aut bitumine coniunctis componenda erit qualiter per exempla posituri sumus: Quandoque vero est usus imaginis vel charapteris et motus per aposita vel aliud intra corpus immissum: sic cum diluiter imago scorpionis in aqua exhibetur adversus venenum aut proprie lapillum in renibus aut similes causas: Tunc non dubitandum erit si fuerit impressio in materia quae ex natura repugnat accidenti, ut in tiriaca aut mitridato adversus renalem lapillum, apparebit vero motus fortior.

...

GIORGIO ANSELMI / *Brian Johnson*

[121r]

and herbs, though these do not last like minerals do.
But, it is not for us at present
to discuss the natures and properties of minerals. No matter how
many more planets may be augmenting the power of a composition's image,
the motive (one), however, is
foremost, just as it is the stronger of them. Therefore by extension
the material shall correspond to it: hence if an image is to be crafted
for two or more distinct things, the material shall be
of conjoined metals, or a mixture of ground gemstones or
those joined with bitumen, as
we will shortly present through examples. At times, however,
an image or character and its motive force is used by means of
application, or otherwise introduced into the body, as when
the image of a scorpion, dissolved in water, is administered
to counter venom, or especially for a kidney stone,
or similar cases. Hence it is not to be doubted
that if an impression is made in a material which by nature
repels certain accidents, as in theriac or mithridatium[15]
to combat a kidney stone, then it indeed provides
a stronger motive force.

...

---

15 Putative universal curatives. Theriac (sometimes known as *mithridatium* after the Pontic king Mithridates, famous for his toxicological endeavors) was primarily an antivenom, known in various forms since the third or fourth century BCE, and often incorporating serpent flesh as an ingredient. See Mayor, 2010: 239–47; Rubin, 2014.

Capitulum quintum Modi imaginum reportarum
in Gemmis quibusdam et eorum posse:

<R>eperiuntur in mineralibus quibusdam
imagines anatura impresse: haec quidem superiorum vires declarant in lapide dragos nominato est serpentis imago: extrahitur autem hic lapis secundum qui philosophi perhibent ex capite
serpentis viventis adhuc et palpitantis, cui principium est posse serpentum morsibus et veneno re-
sistere: et est mirabile quod eius praesentia non plus mo-

CHAPTER FIVE: *The Manners of Images Found in Certain Gemstones, and Their Powers.*

Images imprinted by nature are found in certain minerals;
indeed, in this way
the powers above reveal in the stone called *dragos*[16]
the image of a serpent. And this stone is extracted,
according to what the philosophers say, from the head
of a serpent even as it is alive and moving, the principal power of which
is to resist the bites and venom of serpents.
And it is marvelous how by its presence a serpent will cease to move,

---

16 The *dracontia*, a legendary stone said to form from the brains of dragons. See Pliny, *Natural History* 37.57; Albertus, *Book of Minerals* II.ii.4, "draconites".

<vendis> serpens quasi si mortuus esset: quin ad mortem percussus
neque movetur in adversum: Sunt siquidem mine-
ralia mirabiles habentia virtutes et posse con-
sequentes motum superioris orbis et vim et naturam: apparent insuper concordes in motibus et
accidentium complexionis et fortis posse quam
docet rerum experientia magistra: testes sunt naturales scientie de vegetabilibus et animalibus et
earum partibus: Non mirandum ergo videbitur
si in eis fuerint similitudines impresse suis temporibus duplicantur ad modum posse: minus etenim
mirabile videbitur quod imago serpentis anatura
in nominato lapillo impressa liberat aveneno et
morsu serpentum pariter et imago serpentarii ab
arte composita aut scorpionis imago quondam caro tyri
aut caro scorpionis: haec siquidem carnes amedicis
venena posita sunt et penitus humane vite ini-
micantia: Amplius autem animalia hoc viventia
corpori occurrunt imprimentia intus vel extra<.>
Quae autem similitudo cadit inter tyri carnem et
eius venenum par inter illius imaginem et venenum, qualis inter magnetem et ferrum quisvis de
natura sit gravius, non modo sistitur illius praesentia
motus ad locum gravium, verum in adversum mo-

GIORGIO ANSELMI / Brian Johnson

[127v]

as if it were dead—without beating it to death!—
nor will it be roused to aggression. For minerals
have marvelous virtues and abilities due to
the movement and power and nature of the sphere above.
Moreover, they appear to harmonize (with it) in their movements, and
accidents of complexion, and the force of their power, as
mistress experience teaches of things;
the sciences of plants and animals and
their parts are natural witnesses (to this effect). Therefore it is not to be wondered at
if likenesses should be imprinted in minerals at their (proper) times,
duplicated insofar as possible; less
to be wondered at, in fact, if the image of a serpent imprinted by nature
in the aforesaid stone—just as the image of Serpentarius composed by art, or the image of a scorpion sometimes (appearing in) the flesh of the tyrus (serpent)[17]
or the flesh of a scorpion—should likewise deliver (one) from the venom and
bite of a serpent. Hence the flesh of these creatures is applied by doctors
against venoms, and everything inimical to human life.
And again, the bodies of living animals
come to be thus imprinted both internally and externally.
That similitude, however, which occurs between the flesh of the tyrus and
its venom just as between its image and the venom,
is like (the way that) between a magnet and some iron
there is naturally a greater gravity, instituted not by means of (the iron)
being moved to a place of greater gravity, but rather moved opposite (the magnet),

---

17 A quasi-legendary snake ascribed to the region of Jericho, the flesh of which was used in preparing the theriac remedy. The name appears to derive from a misinterpretation of the Greek word θηρίον in relation to the use of snake flesh as a component of theriac; see Rubin, 2014.

Divinum Opus de Magia Disciplina

[128r]

vetur et ad omnem positionis differentiam convertitur et huius causa est omnifaria inter ea convenientia: sic fit cum fuerit caro tyri aut eius imago et venenum eius praesens quiescit equidem et illud est propter proportionem quae cadit inter illa et vivens tyrus: fortassis vero movetur ad naturam cognitas carnem actione in corpus dimissa. Signum vero huius est qui narrat Albertus magnus in mineralibus qui lapis nominatus repertus est per servos nobilis cuiusdam postquam interfecisent serpentes plurimos invicem conglomeratos et inter eos fuit serpens maior apud quem erat lapis et evaserunt interfectores illesi et immotis serpentibus: accidit autem hoc propter lapidis eius proprietatem ad cuius praesentiam convenerant ex admirabili et intrinseca amicitia et convenientia: Fortassis vero dubitandum videbitur, sunt ne imagines exsectantes in suis motibus benignarum aut malignarum stellarum motum natura aut arte impresse sint et hoc propter laudatos illorum effectus: sed sunt superiorum imagines quibus similes fiant sectantes {illorum}[18] malignam naturam et posse, non dubitamus has imagines sectari naturam et motum supercelestium corporum quorum ad similitudinem sunt impresse qui autem laudandi effectus et motus illam sequuntur

---

18 Redacted in the manuscript, evidently a copyist's error.

and alternated through every different position,
and this is why there is everywhere a symmetry between them.
So it is with the flesh of the tyrus or its image;
its presence indeed neutralizes venom,
because of the symmetry which occurs between it and the living
tyrus, though perhaps (the venom) is moved toward the familiar nature of the flesh
by the act of releasing (that flesh) into the body. But the proof of this
is what Albert the Great relates in his *On Minerals*,[19] that
the aforementioned stone was found by the servants of a certain noble
after they had killed a great many serpents all gathered about one another,
and among them was a larger serpent bearing
a stone, and the slayers escaped unharmed and unshaken
by the serpents; and this occurred because a property of the serpent's stone
had drawn (the others) to its presence by an amazing
and intrinsic affinity and harmony. However, will it not perhaps
appear doubtful that there are images, imprinted by nature or art, which follow
in their movements the movement of the benign or malign stars, and are
thus praised for their effects? But we do not doubt that there are
images made in the likenesses of the (things) above, following a malign
nature and power. These images
follow the nature and movement of the supercelestial bodies[20]
in similitude of which they are imprinted,
yet the effects and movements following upon

---

19 The anecdote is briefly recounted in Albertus, *Book of Minerals* II.ii.4, "draconites".

20 Here presumably referring to the images of the tropical signs themselves, as distinct from the constellations bearing their names. Note, however, that in at least some schools of Hermetic cosmological thought, the decans were also understood to stand above the fixed stars: "Underneath…are arranged the thirty-six decans, in between the circle of the universe <and> that of the zodiac, dividing both circles…Let us consider that the decans preside as guardians…over all things in the cosmos." (from Stobaean Hermetic excerpt VI, in Litwa, trans., 2018: 54).

Divinum Opus de Magia Disciplina

[128v]

praesentiam est accidentale: Turi caro siquidem lepram
curat propter qui inest illorum natura adeuntem
propellendi humores corruptos: Idem scorpionis efficit
caro cum loco punture illius illinita sit et cum
veneni atractiva qualiter est venenum ad illum
mobile: et inest scamonee febrem tertianam curare et colericum humorem educere et infrigidare: cum
tamen eam intermedie demas gradus quarti calefaci-
entes et exsiccantes ponant periti medici: simile est
de pluribus aliis medicinis quas medici begoardicas
nominant et item solutivas quae sive atrahendo sive
evacuando aut resolvendo aut confortando cor
vel expellendo vel quomodo vis operando avene-
nis et infirmitatibus liberant non per patentes qualitates, sed insuper insunt eis vires quibus nocent
quibusdam membris corporis etiam principalibus
propterea coguntur medici admiscere cum eis medi-
cinas bonas resistentes illarum nocumentis et confort-
antes membra quibus apta sunt nocere, ne impressiones suscipiant: ad hunc modum est ars componendi imagines: etenim cum oportuna fuerit compositio cuiusdam ad hos effectus, consideret artifex
horam quam quedam de stellis natura benignis
et foelix sub ea decurrat imagine et maligna natura

their presence, for which they are praised, are accidental. The flesh of the tyrus therefore
cures leprosy because it is in its nature to
be impelled toward corrupt humors; the flesh of the scorpion works likewise
when the location of (the scorpion's) puncture is anointed, and
it attracts the venom just as the venom is made movable toward it;
and scammony is able to cure the tertian fever,
and draw out and cool the choleric humor,
at least when (this plant) is applied by skilled doctors in order to moderate heating and drying of the fourth degree.[21] It is the same with the many other medicines which doctors call "begoardics",
and also laxatives, the power of which works either by extracting or
evacuating or releasing, or by strengthening the heart,
or expelling or the like, to deliver (one) from venoms
and infirmities, not (only) by means of (the medicines') manifest qualities,
but also by those powers in them by which they harm
certain members of the body; indeed it is principally
for that reason that doctors are compelled to mix them with good medicines
which counter their harmful effects and strengthen
the members in which they are apt to cause harm, lest (those parts of the body)
suffer their impression. The art of composing images is after this (same) manner:
for when it is opportune to compose
something for such effects as these, the artificer considers
the hour such that some stars of a benign and fortunate nature
travel under that (celestial) image, and (those of) a malign nature

---

21 Alluding to the theoretical quantitative measure of elemental qualities, such as those imparted by the humors.

cadat quatenus imago iuvativa sit et non nociva<.>
Rursus autem fortassis dubitandum videbitur sunt
ne harum imaginum perpetue vires, aut saltem tempore quanto perdurat figura imaginis in gemma
et hoc ideo quam scriptum est ab antiquorum quibusdam si inventa sit talis imago in tali lapillo, erit
eius motus supra has res et accidentia et hoc videbitur dicendum fore nullius imaginis sive sit ad
generales rerum motus quas maiores admovent radices sive quas particulares aut alie potest esse per-
petua vis: neque rursus quantum perdurat imaginis impressa figura: etenim maiorum et fortissima-
rum constellationum generales radices habent li-
brata suorum motuum tempora, quibus alie alterius et diversi motus succedunt sicut sufficienter
monstravimus in praemissis et sunt succedentes fortes et deficiunt regna et secte et subcedunt alia et
gentes et populi: unde fit necesse ut deficiant pariter cum illis motus imaginum quae in earum vigo-
re sunt impresse et insuper imagines impresse, cito
permutant loca sub orbe novo: ex quibus insuper
palam fit qui non sunt omnes paris motus et virtutis ac posse omni tempore perdurationis: quod
quidem accidit quotiens evenit ut in temporibus

GIORGIO ANSELMI / Brian Johnson

[129r]

are cadent, so that the image is helped and not harmed.
But will it not also perhaps appear doubtful that
the powers of these images are perpetual, or at least enduring
as long as the form of the image in the gemstone?
And like what is written by some of the ancients,
that if a certain image is found in a certain stone it shall
bear a motive (power) over things and accidents (of that nature)?
   And
it will be argued that this is observed of no image, either that it is
a mover of general things—which are driven by the greater roots—
or that it can be a perpetual power of particular things or any others.
Nor, for that matter, does (its power) endure as long as
the imprinted form of the image, for the general roots of the greater
   and most powerful
constellations have balanced
the seasons of their movements, which other (things) of different
and diverse movements follow—just as we have sufficiently
demonstrated in the preceding—and the strong rise,
and kingdoms and sects fall, and
nations and peoples and others pass away. Whence it is necessary
   that
the movements of those images which are imprinted with the vigor
   of those (roots) should likewise fail, and also those (of) imprinted
   images
the places of which under the (celestial) sphere are soon to be ex-
   changed for new ones. Whence, moreover, it is made plain that
   all do not endure with the same movement and virtue
and power in every season, which
indeed is the case when it happens that in their seasons

suis superveniant constellationes fortes et adverse sed contrarii motus cum maxime fuerit motus per directionem principii et per profectionem concordes cum adversa praesente constellatione vel quotiens tandem hylegialis locus figurationis ad abscindens perductus fuit: ideoque nihil admirandum prorsus videbitur si nullum de ydolis in temporibus antiquorum quae nominavimus responsa dantibus iam non appa-

strong and opposing constellations overtake (their predecessors), but
(these superseding) movements are especially contrary when, according to
primary direction and profection,[22] they are harmonious with the presence of an opposing constellation, or, finally, when the place of the hyleg[23] in a (horoscopic) figure has been conducted to (the place of) separation.[24]
And so it is certainly not to be wondered at if none of the idols of ancient times, which we have called givers of oracles, appear any longer;[25]

---

22 Primary directions and profections comprise a variety of methods for calculating the places of planets, house cusps, and other degrees in a chart which is constructed by progressing their natal positions forward in time at a given rate relative to the actual number of years elapsed in the native's life; see de Vore, 2002, s.v. These techniques, known to Hellenistic astrologers in late antiquity, were further developed and transmitted to the medieval Latin West by Arabic intermediaries; see Bezza, 2015: 8–9.
23 A planet or degree in a nativity that is calculated to have a deterministic bearing upon the length of the native's life. See Lewis, 2003: 344–8.
24 Possibly referring to the *alcocoden*, a planet dignified in the degree of the hyleg and aspecting it; Eric Purdue, personal communication.
25 Presumably an allusion to the temple statues described in the *Asclepius* (§ 23–4, 37–8), one of the few Hermetic discourses available to Latin readers before the late fifteenth century, e.g.: "I mean statues ensouled and conscious, filled with spirit and doing great deeds; statues that foreknow the future and predict it by lots, by prophecy, by dreams and by many other means..." (Copenhaver, trans., 1992: 81). These same passages were independently preserved—and propagated to a broad Christian audience for centuries to come—in book VIII of Augustine's *De civitate dei*, where they are quoted in service of his polemic against pagan religions. Hermes does, in fact, suggest a celestial component in the composition and operation of those oracular images, consonant with Anselmi's general theory of correspondence between terrestrial and heavenly things: "[The quality of those gods who are considered earthly] comes from a mixture of plants, stones and spices, Asclepius, that have in them a natural power of divinity. And this is why those gods are entertained with constant sacrifices, with hymns, praises and sweet sounds in tune with heaven's harmony: so that the heavenly ingredient enticed into the idol by constant communication with heaven may gladly endure its long stay among humankind." (Copenhaver, trans., 1992: 90).

reant. Idem penitus erit iudicium de gemmarum
virtutibus in quibus impresse sunt: erit autem gemmarum posse et principium sive radix veluti nata-
litia cum primus eterrae visceribus est producta aut
aquis in lucem: et hoc fortassis decipit quosdam qui
sunt opinati qui gemmae unica vice virtutem suam
effundant et non ultra qui non earum proprietates
famosas grandes viderunt: ea propter dicebant
zaphirum, unum carbunculum curare solum
eius tamen experientiam ad contrarium ipsius
vidimus: Quanvis enim quinque non curet, non pro-
ptera dicendum erit non esse illi vigorem sive pre-
dictas causas vel fortassis erit ex parte recipien-
tis non apti sicut plerunque medicantibus evenit
et non substantia gemmae quae semel anaturali co-
lore passa virtute sua spolietur, qualiter terre

nascentia plurima.

GIORGIO ANSELMI / Brian Johnson

[129v]

the judgment will be quite the same concerning the virtues of gemstones
in which imprints are made. But there is
a power in gemstones, and its principle or root is the same as
that of newborns, when the entrails are first animated out of earth or
water, and perhaps this deceives those who
are of the opinion that gemstones only pour out their virtue one single time
and never again, who have not seen their great and famous properties. For they say that
a sapphire only cures a carbuncle once,
but we have seen an experiment with it to the contrary;
indeed, it may not cure some one in five (people)—not because,
as will be claimed, that is not its power—either due to preexisting conditions,
or perhaps that the patient is not fit to receive it,
as is often the case with medicines,
and not because the substance of the gemstone, which by natural constitution
has one time spread out its virtue, should then be stripped of it, like

[130r]

many things born of the earth.

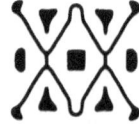

[*The following is from MS Vat. lat. 5333, with emendations based on MS Plut. 44.35*]

[iv]

Quarta pars, quarti Tractatus Georgii
parmensis, De modis specialibus
Imaginum octavi Orbis. Et de modis
compositionum earumdem
per exempla.

THE FOURTH PART OF THE FOURTH TRACTATE OF
GEORGE OF PARMA, ON THE SPECIFIC METHODS
PERTAINING TO *the Images of the Eighth
Sphere,* AND ON THE METHODS OF THEIR
COMPOSITION, BY MEANS OF EXAMPLES.

De Imaginibus, quae fiunt ex signis .12. Zodiaci. Capitulum primum.

Sufficienter in praemissis, modus per exempla completus est, imagines componendi, quae fiunt super radices tam minores, quam maiores, et medias, communes, et appropriatas. et si cum his posite sunt quaedam ex .8º. orbe assumpte, volumus tamen poneremus speciales modos quibus .8^i. huius orbis imagines componendae sunt, et quas res, et accidentia habent movere. Est autem in universalibus monstratus, quae signum unum quidque zodiaci gubernat res huius mundi inferioris, et accidentia similia naturae, et significationis suae. Et item imagines reliquae. Nec modo haec, verum et quas philosophi Egyptii, et persae et babilonici, et graeci, atque indi, diverunt concomitari .12. signa zodiaci, et imagines reliquas .36. numero, stellatas, quae exeuntes zodiacum pinguntur, cum ad exortum perveniunt, aut ad summum caelum, aut ad occiduua, et nos posimus

GIORGIO ANSELMI / Brian Johnson

[1r]

CHAPTER ONE: *On the Images Which Are Made According to the Twelve Signs of the Zodiac.*

It is sufficient to begin with the complete method, by means of examples,
of composing images which are made
based upon the roots, the minor as well as the major and the middling,
the common and the particular. And if it is the case that, when these
are in place, something is received from the eighth sphere,[26] we wish
nonetheless to set down specific methods by which
the images of this eighth sphere are composed, and what
things and accidents they move. It is, however,
universally demonstrated that
each one of the signs of the Zodiac governs the things of this world
below, and likewise the accidents of nature, and their significations.
And likewise the remaining images—not
only these (aforementioned), but also those that the philosophers of
the Egyptians, Persians,
Babylonians, Greeks, and Indians have said
accompany the twelve signs of the Zodiac, and the remaining stellar images,
thirty-six in number, which are depicted outside the Zodiac—
(do so) when they become visible, or reach the midheaven,
or upon their setting, and we have put

---

26 I.e., automatically, or by their own power.

in locis illis tabulas, secundum quas facile scitis
loca sub quae nono orbe decurrunt. habetur
quo sub eius loco peroriuntur, summum tenentes caelum, et occiduas partes. Restat hic nobis
prosequi imaginum harum componendarum tempera,
et quas res, et accidentia moveant cum compositae
fiunt. Est vero generale, quotiens ex
harum quavis perfectum intendimus, sub ea
decurrat alterum luminum, et hora compositionis
horoscopet, et sit lumen ipsum benignis, et
foelicibus vallatus stellis, aut saltem ea decurrat
sub imagine fortis, foelix, et benigna, quae
quidem mane in exortu solem praecedat, in nocte
lunam, cadant malignae, et dominatrices lo-
corum quae res adversas, et inimica gubernant
accidentia. sit quoque stella haec quae natura rem
aut intentum accidens movet, et regulat. Contra
cum fuerit ad nocendum imago, decurrat sub
ea tempore compositionis eius maligna, et infoelix

[1v]

these down in tables of their places, following which it is easy for you to know
the places through which they move beneath the ninth sphere, having
the place under which they rise, attain the midheaven,
and the place where they set.[27] It remains here for us
to describe the composition of these images which you are to assemble,
and what things and accidents they shall move when
they are composed. It is generally true, whenever
we intend to bring about anything by means of one of these (images), that
one luminary or the other shall be moving under it, and rising in the hour of the composition,
and that the luminary shall be unafflicted, and
fortified by fortunate stars, or at least moving
under an image that is strong, fortunate, and beneficent, which
in any case rises before the Sun at dawn, (or) at night
(before) the Moon. The malefics shall be cadent, and (also) the lords of the houses
which are adverse to the matter of concern, and which govern inimical
accidents. Thus shall be each star which by nature
moves and regulates the thing or intended accident. Conversely,
when an image is to be made to cause injury,
a malign and infortunate (star) shall rise under that one at the time of its composition,

---

27 Anselmi does not, in fact, appear to include any such tables in the *Divinum opus*, nor in the known extant copy of the *Astronomia*.

horoscopet, et stella maligna haec regulet
et moveat accidens intentum ex natura, et sit
dominatrix loci, qui natura hoc gubernat accidens.
vel sit haec stella dominatrix loci moventis accidens, maligna natura adiuncta stellae motrici
dictae ex diametro, vel tetragono, cadant benignae, et debiles sint impeditae. est autem
particulariter de unoquoque dicendum.
ARIETIS IMAGO quotiens ad bona di-
rigitur accidentia, confortat animantia omnia
quae signum gubernat, proprie autem, et magis, domestica, minuta, nostra subiugalia,
neque equitabilia, speciem ovinam, caprinam,
porcinam, et similes. Caput confortat, et
ab aegritudinibus praeservat, praecipue quidem
oculorum, defedationibus cutis, et leprae.
Confortat quoque hominum exercitia, et operationes,
quae sunt de eius gubernatione, vel ex patria, vel ex radice natalia, aut eius

and this malign star shall regulate
and move the intended accident by (its) nature, and shall be
lord of the house which by nature governs this accident.
Or, the star which is lord of the house moving the accident
shall be malign by nature, aspecting the aforementioned motive stars
by opposition, or square. The benefics shall be cadent,
and debilitated with impediment.[28] Yet it remains
to speak of each one in particular.
THE IMAGE OF ARIES, when it is directed toward a good
accident, strengthens every creature
governed by the sign, but particularly, and more greatly,
the domesticated, the small, those we put under the yoke,
not fit for riding, of the form of sheep, goats,
swine and the like. It strengthens the head, and
protects against illnesses, especially
of the eyes, corruptions of the skin, and leprosy.
It also strengthens the occupations and activities of people
who are governed by it, either due to (their) birthplace,
or natal root, or according to their

---

28 That is, in a sign of the planet's fall or detriment (debility), and badly aspected (impediment).

annua conversione, aut in quibus ad eum pervenit
motus ab horoscopo, vel ab hilegiali loco
directionis, et item profectionis. Confortat item
reges, et dignatores, et nobiles, et exercituum duces.
Et si pro locis in quibus metalla nascuntur fiant
imagines abundare faciunt his. Et rursus
confortat loca omnia, praecipue cum gubernaverit
ea signum pro quibus impressa fuerit. Excitat
rursus, et vigorat corpora humana, et animantia
cetera quorum est complexio attinens cholerae, etenim
signum est illius gubernator naturae. Ideoque imago,
flegmate abundantibus superfluo, pro utilis est ad
curam, et aegritudinum quae ex ea fiunt. Et si
ad ventos, aut ad demones fiat, movet
quae suae sunt partis, et universaliter res omnes
quae sub ea sunt gubernatione, vigorat, et
confortat. Est autem compositionis modus, et temporibus,
cum sub hoc imagine, proprie quidem sub gradu qui Solis
honor ponitur decurrit sol, et est eius .19. gradus.

[2v]

annual (solar) return, or according to those (influences)[29] which
reach the sign, having been moved from the ascendant, or from the place of the hyleg,
by direction or profection. It likewise strengthens
kings, and dignitaries, and nobles, and leaders of soldiers.
And if images (of it) are fashioned in places where metals grow,
they make these abundant. But for that matter
it strengthens all places, particularly when they are governed
by the sign for which the image has been imprinted. It also excites
and invigorates the human body, and other creatures
which usually have a choleric complexion, since
the sign naturally governs that temperament: therefore, an image
overflowing with phlegmatic abundance is useful for
curing (individuals of that temperament), and illnesses caused by it. And if
the image is made for winds or demons, it moves
those of this sign's region,[30] and in general
invigorates and strengthens all things which are under its governance.
And the method and time of its composition
are when the Sun travels under this image, particularly under the degree of the Sun's
exaltation, and that is the nineteenth degree.

---

29 Namely, of degrees—such as that of the ascendant or hyleg—progressed from the natal chart.

30 Elsewhere (Plut. 44.35, 47v), Anselmi notes that the subordinate things which celestial powers govern via demonic agents include geographic regions: "...the power and activity of the demons of Saturn is principally in the parts of the world which Saturn moves...".

Luna autem sub ♌ illi trigona, et Iupiter, et
Mars ambo sub ♐ iuncti, et ipsi Soli
trigoni, aut Mercurius sub signo ♓ decurrens retrorsus incedat, et .12. teneat locum
sub ♉ Venus, Luna tetragona cum ♃, cadant
Saturnus, et Cauda. Siquidem tenet summum Sol caelum, Venus initia teneat .XI. et
cum ♃ Mars sub ♐ trigoni Soli, et Luna
suo loco dicto. Haec impressa cum summum tenet
caelum Sol, fortior creditur quidam cum horoscopat,
dumtaxat regibus, et dignitates volentibus. Sit
vero imaginis figura qualem diximus assignari in
orbe. Dicunt quidam, lingua careat, et imprimatur, vel potius fundatur in auro, vel argento,
aut imprimatur in quadam ex gemmis ad hanc
intentionem, et est alectorius praecipuus, et ceterae
quas diximus benignarum sectari motus.
Siquidem intendit artifex eius compositionem ad nocendum, et inimicandum potentibus, sit impressio

GIORGIO ANSELMI / Brian Johnson

[3r]

And the Moon in Leo shall be trine the Sun, and Jupiter and
Mars both joined in Sagittarius trine the Sun.
Or, Mercury in the sign of Pisces shall be moving
retrograde, and Venus shall occupy the twelfth house
under Taurus, the Moon and Jupiter squaring it.
Saturn and Cauda Draconis shall be cadent. However, if the Sun
 occupies the midheaven,
Venus shall occupy the beginning of the eleventh house, and
Jupiter and Mars under Sagittarius shall be trine the Sun, and the
 Moon
shall be in its aforementioned place. This image is imprinted when
the Sun occupies the midheaven—more effectively, some believe,
 when it rises—
insofar as the rulers and dignities allow.
But the form of the image shall be as we have said it is arranged in
the (celestial) sphere, some say without a tongue, and it is engraved,
or alternatively cast, in gold or silver,
or engraved in some gemstone suitable for this purpose,
and especially the *alectoria*, and others
which we have said follow the movement of the benign (stars).
However, if the artificer intends that their composition
have the power to cause injury and make enemies, it shall be
 imprinted

quotiens ♄ sub ea decurrit horoscopans
cum ♋, ambo vero ♃ et ☿ sub ♋ tetragoni, ☽ Saturno diametra, sub ♍ ☉ ♂ ☿ cum eo.
IMAGO ♉ EST EIUS VIS, ET POSSE
quotiens impressa fuit in horis quas dicemus.
Potens est, et confortat animalia grossa, domestica
subiugalia, equitabilia, proprie vero species bo-
vinas, et homines. Item quorum gubernator signum
ex radice, aut annuali conversione, et motu
profectionis, aut directionis in ipsum, eorum quidem
exercitia, et operationes quorum pro hylarem, et volup-
tuosam ducunt vitam. Praeservat item corporis
membra quae sub sua sunt gubernatione, collum
et adiacentes partes, et curat ab aegritudinibus
melancholicis, et a partibus eius materiae, et
item a morbis oculorum, dicuntque ab his quae
epati et felli superveniunt. Confortat rursus
loca omnia quorum gubernator est signum, aut
accidenti cum ex edificatione, vel natura culta, et

when Saturn rises under this sign
with Cauda Draconis, but both Jupiter and Venus[31] under Cancer
    square it.
The Moon shall be under Virgo, together with the Sun, Mars, and
    Mercury, opposing Saturn.
THE IMAGE OF TAURUS has its strength and power
when it is imprinted in the hours which we shall relate.
It is powerful, and strengthens animals that are large, domesticated,
put under the yoke, fit for riding, but particularly bovine species,
and likewise those humans whom the sign governs
natally, or according to their annual (solar) return, or due to (an
    influence)
reaching it by profection or direction. Indeed, to it belong
the occupations and activities which lead one's life toward cheerful-
    ness and pleasure.
Likewise it preserves the members of the body
which are governed by it, the neck
and adjacent parts. And it cures melancholic illnesses
and their causes, and
likewise diseases of the eyes, and they say that among these (illness-
    es) are included those
that come upon the liver and gall bladder. But for that matter it
    strengthens
all places and accidents of which this sign is governor, whether
cultivated naturally or by artifice, and

---

31 The copyist of Vat. lat. 5333 erroneously drew the sigil for Mercury in two different places in the instructions for this hypothetical chart. I suspect the first instance should actually be Venus, given that this would place the two benefics (Venus and Jupiter) together, and that Mercury is more likely to be found nearer the Sun.

Divinum Opus de Magia Disciplina

terrae nascentia omnia, proprie arbores grandes,
et perdurantes, quarum sunt fructus terrei, sti-
ptici, et insipidi. Excitat item, et vigorat qualitates personarum, quarum signum gubernat fri-
gitatem, et siccitatem, hinc fit utilis imago
cum timentur putridorum humorum febres, et pesti-
ferae. movet rursus ventos, et item demones,
partis quam gubernat, et universaliter res omnes, et accidentia gubernationis signi. Est autem mo-
dus compositionis, et hora, quotiens sub hac imagine
decurrit Sol, cum ad commoda fit, proprie quidem
sub gradu .3. sub hoc numero fore honorem Lunae te-
stantur philosophi. Venus autem, et ☽, sub ♋, illi exagona. Cum Sole Mercurius, sub ♓ ♃ exago-
nus. cadant cum ☋ malignae. vel ambo ♃
et ☽ sub eo gradu decurrentes horoscopent. Sit
hora alterius eorum sub ♋ Sol, cum ☿, sub
♋ Venus, aut cum ☽ et ♃ malignae cadant
et ☋. Imprimatur imago qualis in orbe figura

everything born of the earth, particularly great and enduring trees,
which bear earthy, astringent,
and tasteless fruits. Likewise it excites and invigorates
the personal qualities which this sign governs, coldness
and dryness, hence the image is useful
in case of the fearsome and pestilential fevers caused by putrid
    humors.
On the other hand, it moves winds, and likewise demons,
of the sort which the sign governs, and in general all the things and
    accidents
governed by it. And the method
and time of its composition are when the Sun travels under this
    image,
when its condition is favorable, particularly
under the third degree, under which number the philosophers
    testify is the exaltation of the Moon.
And Venus and the Moon under Cancer shall be sextile the Sun.
Mercury shall be with the Sun, sextile Jupiter under Pisces.
The malefics shall be cadent along with Cauda Draconis. Or, both
    Jupiter
and the Moon shall rise in that (aforementioned) degree. Should it
    be
a different season, the Sun with Mercury under Cancer,
Venus shall be under Cancer, or with the Moon and Jupiter; the ma-
    lefics and Cauda Draconis shall be cadent.
The image shall be imprinted just as the figure is set in the (celestial)
    sphere:

ponitur, ut sit figura bovis caudae grandis, grandes
oculos, parvuus os, imprimitur in quadam ex gemmis, aut fundit ex auro, aut argento, vel ex
aere. Ad nocendum si fuerit, erit hora, cum
Mars, et ♃ ambo iuncti fuerint sub ea,
Saturnus eis diameter, vel tetragonus, sub ♒
Sol, illis, et ipse tetragonus, aut sub ♑ Saturnus
cadens, Luna cum eis, aut .12. tenens, aut .8.
cum ☋, vel sit cum coniunctus Cauda, vel Saturno,
Venus autem retrorsus incedat excandens Solis radiis.
IMAGO SIGNI ♓ est valida, quotiens
secundum artem composita sit, et potens ad vigorandum
et confortandum, universaliter humanam naturam, et aves
magnas quidem, et domesticas, homines quidem confortat, quorum, et naturam, et accidentia signum
gubernat, quacumque fuerit ex radice, vel an-
nali conversione, et quocumque ex hilegio per-
venerit ad eum motus. Inter homines, aut sapientes, nobiles, et ingeniosos artium, et exercitiorum

it shall be like the figure of a cow with a long tail, big
eyes, and a small mouth, engraved in a gemstone,
or cast from gold or silver, or from
copper. If it is to cause injury, the time shall be when
Mars and Jupiter are both joined under this sign,
Saturn opposing or squaring them, the Sun under Aquarius
also squaring them itself. Or, Saturn shall be cadent under Capricorn,
the Moon there with it or occupying the twelfth or eighth house
together with Cauda Draconis, or conjunct Cauda Draconis or Saturn,
but Venus shall be moving retrograde, burned by the rays of the Sun.

THE IMAGE OF THE SIGN OF GEMINI is strong when
it is composed according to the art, and powerful for invigorating
and strengthening the human nature in general, and
indeed large birds, and domestic ones. In any case, it strengthens people
the nature and accidents of whom the sign also
governs, whether natally, or according to their annual
(solar) return, and also in any case where (an influence) reaches the sign from the hyleg.
Among humans, or intelligent creatures,
(it governs) the noble, and those gifted in the arts, and masters of their occupations.

magistros. membra vero hominis quae signum gubernat, sunt brachia, et spatulae, et adiacentes partes eorum confortat, et adiuvat, et ab aegritudinibus eorum curat, et praeservat, propriae quidem sanguineis, et dicunt quidam splenes. loca rursus, et terras quae et naturas gubernat, accidentiaque excitat, et vigorat terreas qualitates, et calorem, et humorem. et fit figura eius melancholicis conveniens, temperans hyemalem aerem. Movet quoque partis quam gubernat ventos, et demones. Et universaliter accidentia, et res gubernationis eius. Est autem hora compositionis eius, cum Sol sub eo decurrit, proprie quidem sub 30. gradu etenim eo in loco est ☊ honor, et horoscopet ☿, vel recto cursu procedens Soli unitus sit, Luna sub ♍, sub ♈ Caput, cui exagonus sit Sol, sub ♋ Venus, Lunae exagona. malignae cadant. siquidem fuerit ♃ cum ☽, vel cum ☊, non inutilis erit, sed boni motus.

But the members of the human (body) which the sign governs
are the arms and shoulder blades, and
it strengthens and helps their adjacent parts, and
protects and cures them of illnesses, particularly
those of the blood, and some say of the spleen. It also stimulates places
and lands, and natures and accidents which the sign governs.
And it invigorates aerial[32] qualities,
and hotness and wetness, and its figure is
suitable for melancholics, tempering the wintry
air. It also moves winds and demons of the sort which the sign governs,
and in general the accidents and things
governed by it. And the time of its composition is
when the Sun travels under this sign, particularly
the third degree, because in that place is the exaltation of Caput Draconis.
And Mercury shall be ascending, or moving direct in its course
while united with the Sun.[33] The Moon shall be under Virgo. Caput Draconis shall be under Aries,
to which the Sun shall be sextile. Venus shall be under Cancer, sextile to the Moon.
The malefics shall be cadent. But should Jupiter be with the Moon, or
with Caput Draconis, it is not useless, but of good influence.

---

32 Reading, with Plut. 44.35, 199r, *aerias* [from *aereas*] for *terreas*.
33 *soli unitus*; probably implying cazimi, see 20r below.

Dicunt qui sit tortuosi, duorum hominum figura,
umbilicum adusque solius, ad hoc pro inferiores
partes. Funditur vero ex auro, vel argento,
aut imprimitur in quodam ex lappillis appropriatis.
Ad nocendum autem fit cum ♄ et Mars, et ☋, sub
hoc decurrentes signo, horoscopant, sub ♏ Sol,
cum eo Mercurius retrorsus incedens, et cum eis
Venus, Luna vero Soli adiuncta, diametra,
vel tetragona, vel pariter malignis.
IMAGO ♋ confortat, et vigorat animantia
omnia quae signum gubernat, aquatilia, ostreosa,
pari rationes homines quos gubernat secundum modos
antedictos, magis vero sexus foeminei, et
quorum est exercitium partes suae gubernationis, piscatores, nautas, et exercitia reliqua circa aquas, et quae littoribus habitant.
Membera quae signum gubernat praeservat
ab aegritudinibus, et factorum adiuvat curam
et addunt quidam ventris aegritudines, certe autem

GIORGIO ANSELMI / Brian Johnson

They say that it should be a twisted figure of two humans
sharing one midsection, to which are added the lower
parts. And it is cast from gold or silver,
or engraved in an appropriate stone.
But to cause injury it shall be made when Saturn and Mars and
    Cauda Draconis
rise under this sign. The Sun shall be under Scorpio,
together with Mercury moving retrograde, and with them
Venus, but the Moon shall be conjunct, opposing,
or square the Sun, or aspecting the malefics likewise.
THE IMAGE OF CANCER strengthens and invigorates all creatures
that the sign governs: aquatic ones, oysters,
and likewise those rational humans it governs according to the
    manners
aforesaid—but moreso the female sex—and
the sorts of occupations governed by it,
fishers, sailors, and the rest of the occupations
around the water, and those residing on the shore.
This sign protects the (bodily) members it governs
from illnesses, and helps in the making of a cure,
and assists somewhat with illnesses of the stomach, but surely

oculorum, et pruritus, et scabiem, et lepram, et
alopetiam. universaliter autem cutis foedationes. loca
rursus omnia quae natura gubernat, aut accidentia,
et item terrae nascentia, quae circa aquas crescunt,
et in eis. Provocat autem primas quas signum
qualitates gubernat, et frigus, et humores,
propria eius impressio cholericis confert corporibus,
et quae facile in febres cadunt ex cholera genitas,
et aestivum aerem reprimit, et universaliter res omnes, et
accidentia quae signum gubernat, et movet.
Est autem compositionis eius hora, quotiens Sol sub eo
signo decurrens horoscopat, proprie quidem cum sub
.13°. gradu sub quo Iovis est honor, Luna vero
sub ♈ .19. gradu, Iupiter cum ea, aut sub Tauro
ambo exagoni soli, sub ♉ Venus, coniunctis
exagona. malignae cadant, et ☋. aut sub Solis
loco decurrant ☽ et ♃ et horoscopent.
Fiat imago Cancri qualis in orbe descriptione,
fundit ex auro, vel argento, vel sculpitur in gemmis appropriatis.

those of the eyes, and itching, and scabies, and leprosy, and
alopecia, and corruptions of the skin in general.
And again, all places the nature or accident of which it governs,
and likewise things born of the earth, which grow up in and around
    waters.
But it primarily provokes those qualities which the sign
governs, and coldness and wetness,
its impression particularly binding the choleric (humor) in bodies,
and (symptoms) which readily befall in fevers engendered by choler,
and it represses the summer air, and in general (provokes) all things
    and
accidents which the sign governs and moves.
And the time of its composition is when the Sun
rises under this sign, particularly when it is under
the thirteenth degree, under which Jupiter is exalted, but the Moon
is under the nineteenth degree of Aries, together with Jupiter, or
both of them under Taurus sextile the Sun. Venus under Taurus
    shall apply to
a sextile (with the Sun). The malefics and Cauda Draconis shall be
    cadent. Or,
the Moon and Jupiter shall rise in the house of the Sun.
The image of Cancer is made as described in the (celestial) sphere,
cast from gold or silver, or sculpted in an appropriate gemstone.

Est rursus commoda regibus, et potentibus. Ad nocendum autem potens est, cum facta sit malignis adiunctis sub ea decurrentibus, et si horoscopant. Sol autem illis diameter, et retrorsus eorum uterque moveatur, sub ♓ Luna. Venere, et Mercurio cum Sole. Iupiter cum Luna, aut sub ♒. vel sit malignorum altera horoscopans, et altera illi tetragona, et erit fortis. Imprimitur autem in ferro, aut funditur in plumbo, aut in aliqua ex gemmis qui malignorum sectantur motus.
IMAGO ♌. cum et ipsa fit secundum ordinem dicendum, est potens, et valida, vigorans res omnes quas signum gubernat, animalia, feras praecipue sylvestres, hasque indomabiles, praecipue quidem leones. Confortat item homines quos omnes signum gubernat, sive accidenti, sive naturae, et per motus iam dictos ex eorum radicibus. Rursus exercitia quae gubernat, et operationes, et actus, movet ad honores, et dignitates,

GIORGIO ANSELMI / Brian Johnson

[6v]

It is also advantageous for kings and potentates.
It is powerful in causing injury, however, when made with the conjoined malefics
rising in this sign,
but the Sun opposing them, and both of them moving retrograde.
The Moon shall be under Gemini, Venus and Mercury
with the Sun. Jupiter shall be with the Moon, or under Aquarius. Or,
one of the malefics shall be rising, and the other
squaring it, and it will be strong. And it is imprinted in
iron, or cast in lead, or in a
gemstone which follows the movement of the malign (stars).
THE IMAGE OF LEO, when it is made according to
the order stated, is powerful and strong, invigorating
all things that the sign governs: animals,
especially woodland beasts, the untameable ones, (and) particularly
lions. It likewise strengthens all those people whom
the sign governs, whether by accident or by nature,
and by the influence of their nativities as already stated.
On the other hand, it moves toward honors and dignities the occupations and activities
and behaviors which it governs,

Divinum Opus de Magia Disciplina

ad officia, et regna his aptos, et ad famam,
et hoc quidem amplius quorum in radicibus summum
coelum tenuerit, aut cum ab eo loco in ipsum
est motus per profectionem, vel directionem.
Reges autem et potentes quorum est gubernator
exaltat, magnificat, honorat, famosas facit,
et item exercitium dures. Membra vero quae sub
sua sunt gubernatione cor, et stomachum confortat, praeservat, et factas curar aegritudines,
et item oculorum. omnia rursus loca quae natura
gubernat, aut accidenti signum exaltat, et
fama auget. excitat item qualitates quas
signum gubernat, et vigorat fortassis, praeter
modum, calorem cum sicitate. Idioque ex accidenti
corpora vigorat ea in quibus flegmata praeter
modum generantur nocentia, et facientia cadere
in infirmitates, et aegritudines, et curationi eorum
apta. Rursus autem movet, et provocat partem
mundi quam gubernat ventos, et demones,

toward offices and rulerships appropriate to these, and toward fame,
and indeed thus moreso in those for whom the sign occupies the
 midheaven natally,
or when (an influence) from that place reaches the sign by progression or direction.
And kings and potentates of whom it is governor
it exalts, glorifies, honors, makes famous,
and likewise makes their undertakings endure. But
it strengthens and preserves and effects cures for illnesses of the
 (bodily) members which the sign governs, the heart and stomach,
and likewise the eyes. The sign also exalts and augments the fame of
 every place which by nature or accident it governs. And it excites
 the qualities which
the sign governs, and invigorates—perhaps excessively—
hotness and dryness. Likewise
it reinvigorates bodies from circumstances in which phlegm
generated beyond moderation injures them, or causes
infirmities and illnesses to befall them, and it cures them
appropriately. On the other hand, it moves and provokes
the winds and demons of that part of the world which it governs;

universaliter quidem quascumque res, et accidentia signum
    gubernat,
movet, at adducit. Est autem compositionis
eius hora, quotiens eo sub signo Sol decurrit
maxime quidem cum sub stella, primam sorta magnitudinem, quae cordi inscribitur, et dicitur Cor, sive
Rex. Patefactus est in antecedentibus quae sub gradu
orbis .8.[i] decurrens, in praesenti autem ad exortum
pervenit, aut summum attingit coelum. cum itaque
sub eo loco Sol decurrit horoscopans, sub ♐
♃ decurrat, illi trigonus, et cum eo Luna,
ambo vero ☿ et ♀ cum Sole, aut sub ♎, Venus
illi exagona. malignae penitus cadant, et Cauda.
Funditur autem ex auro puro, aut in aliqua ex gemmis
aptis. Scriptum est vero in libello de .15. stellis,
imprimendam fore imago sub ♌ stella decurrente
Sole, cum summum attigerit coelum, laudavit
vero hanc imaginem, et dixit eam deus magnificus
et regales honores, et divitiarum affluentias.
et in granato sculpendam, qui est de genere

[7v]

indeed, generally whatever things and accidents the sign governs,
it moves and attracts. And the time of the image's composition
is when the Sun travels under this sign,
especially when it it under that star of the first magnitude
which is inscribed in its heart, and called "the heart", or
"the king"[34]—it has been disclosed previously under which degree
of the eighth sphere this lies, but for the matter at hand it is rising,
or reaching the midheaven. When, therefore,
the Sun rises under that place, Jupiter shall be traveling under Sagittarius,
trine the Sun, and the Moon shall be with Jupiter.
But both Mercury and Venus shall be with the Sun, or under Libra (with) Venus
sextile the Sun. The malefics shall be entirely cadent, and also Cauda Draconis.
And it is cast from pure gold, or (engraved) in an appropriate gemstone.
But it is written in the book of the fifteen stars[35]
that the image is to be imprinted with the Sun under the star of Leo
when it reaches the midheaven.
Indeed it praises this image, and calls it a god of great
and regal honors, and abundant wealth.
And it is sculpted in garnet, which is a type

---

34 *cor, sive rex*; i.e. Cor Leonis, or Regulus.
35 Presumably *De Quindecim Stellis*, attributed to Hermes.

Carbunculi, et iam notum est hunc eundem
lapillum esse de confortantibus cor, laetificare,
et amovere tristitia, et prohibere eam habet.
Ad regnum commoda commendabilis fortassis
erit quae alectorio fuerit impressa. Figura vero
imaginis sit, et compositionis horam commodat motus
super ex hermete posuimus. Sunt quae figurant
leonem cui insidet homini clamidatus regio ha-
bitu, hic Solem dextra tenet, et sinistra leonis
auriculam. Sunt vero huius sicut, et ceterarum
figurae diversae pro diversitate intentionis artificis.
Ad nocendum fit imago, quotiens altera, aut utraque
malignorum sub eo decurrit, et cum eis ☋,
vel cum Luna, et sit ☽ malignis diametra,
vel tetragona, sub ♓ Sol, ab aliorum conspectu
cadens, Mercurius item cum Luna, radiis excandens
Iupiter, et Venus. Nociva est imago, movens res, et
accidentia narratis adversa. imprimitur vero in ferro, aut
funditur ex plumbo, aut insignitur cuidam ex gemmis quas

of carbuncle, and it should be noted here that this
stone itself strengthens the heart, brings joy,
and takes away sadness and prevents one from holding on to it. Respectable advantages may
accrue to the rule of those who imprint (this image) in the *alectoria* stone. But the form
of the image, and the time of its composition, shall conform to the work
of Hermes we have set down above. Some make a figure
of a lion, upon which sits a person cloaked in royal attire,
holding the Sun in their right hand, and the lion's
ear with their left. But of this, just as the others, there are
diverse figures for the diverse purposes of the artificer.
To cause injury, the image shall be made when one or both
malefics are under this sign, Cauda Draconis with them
or with the Moon, and the Moon opposing
or squaring the malefics. The Sun shall be under Pisces, cadent from any aspect with the others,
and Mercury with the Moon.
Jupiter and Venus shall be burned by the rays (of the Sun). The image does harm by moving things and
accidents contrary to what has been related (in the preceding), and it is imprinted in iron, or
cast from lead, or inscribed in one of the gemstones which

praediximus sequi malignorum motum.
IMAGO ♍ confortat, et fortem facit naturam
humanam, magis vero foemellas quorum in radice
fuerit locus horoscopans, aut annuae conversionis,
vel quando in signum fuerit motus per directionem, aut
profectionem ab hylego. Doctos quoque homines, scribas
et quorum sunt exercitia in naturalibus sciis, et mathematicis. Conservat item, et praeservat corpora
humana ab aegritudinibus, et factis est in adiutorium.
Partium atque quas signum gubernat ventrem, re-
nes, et his adiacentia membra, cumque commovet
qualitates elementales frigidus et sicco, est adiutorium
curae aegritudinum quae a sangue fiunt. Confortat
item, et multiplicat aves, et est illi grandis
proprietas ad multiplicandum terrae nascentia, et
sata, et segetes. steriles facit terras, et loca
quae signum natura, aut accidenti gubernat. utilis
fit temporibus, quibus pestes vigent, putredinibus resi-
stere. Sui gubernationis signi partis ventos,

we have said follow the movement of the malign (stars).
THE IMAGE OF VIRGO strengthens and fortifies the human nature,
but moreso (that of) girls for whom
it is in the ascendant natally, or according to their annual (solar) return,
or because (an influence) reaches the sign by direction
or profection from the hyleg. Learned people as well, scribes,
and those whose occupations are in the natural sciences and mathematics.
Likewise it preserves and protects human bodies
from illnesses, and is fashioned as an aid.
Also, the parts which the sign governs are the stomach, kidneys,
and members adjacent to these. When it excites
the elemental qualities of coldness and dryness, it is an aid
in curing illnesses which are caused by the sanguine humor.
Likewise it strengthens and multiplies birds, and it has the great
quality of multiplying new growth in the earth, and
crops and planted fields. It makes sterile the lands and places
which the sign governs by nature or accident, (so)
it is useful in times when pests flourish, to resist putrefaction.
It rouses winds and attracts demons of the sort governed by the sign.

Divinum Opus de Magia Disciplina

[9r]

commovet, et demones adducit. Est vero
compositionis eius hora, quotiens sub eo signo Sol
decurrit, proprie sub gradu honoris ☿, et est illi
Mercurius unitus, aut ☿ sub eodem gradu cum Sole
decurrens, non excandeat, aut retrorsus incedat eius horoscopat loco Venus, aut ☽ illi
exagona sub ♋, Iupiter trigonus aut exagonus Soli.
malignae cadant, et ☋, et subambulet inferioris stellae signa, non superioris. Figura eius fit
qualiter diximus imaginem in orbe stellato pingi.
Ponunt autem virginis mulieris, panno involutae
leonem equitantis, et dexter tenentis ferreum bacculum.
imprimitur in aliqua ex nominatis gemmis, praecipue
amethisto, vel corneola, berillo, chrisolito,
smaragdo, adamante, aut funditur ex auro
vel argento. et asserunt hanc imaginem fortem
ad faciendis agros uberes, pariter, et domos
in quibus fuerit. Ad nocendum contrario dis-
ponitur modo signum. Damnatur enim praesentia

[9r]

But the time of its composition is when the Sun travels under this sign,
particularly under the degree of Mercury's exaltation,[36] and
Mercury is united with it, or (in any case) is under the same degree as the Sun,
not combust or moving retrograde.
Venus shall be rising in this sign's house, or the Moon
under Cancer shall be sextile to it. Jupiter shall be trine or sextile the Sun.
The malefics and Cauda Draconis shall be cadent, and traveling under
the sign of an inferior star, not a superior one.[37] Its figure shall be
as we have said the image is depicted in the stellar sphere.
In any case, they make (the image) of a virgin woman, wrapped in a garment,
riding a lion, and holding an iron wand in her right hand.
It is imprinted in one of the aforementioned gemstones, particularly
amethyst, or carnelian, beryl, chrysolite,
emerald, diamond, or cast from gold
or silver, and they sow this powerful image
to make fields fruitful, and also homes
in which it is placed. To cause injury, on the contrary,
the sign is arranged in this way: it is condemned by the presence

---

36 15° ♍.
37 Probably referring to signs ruled by the so-called inferior planets, Venus and Mercury, those below the Sun in the classical ordering of the celestial spheres; hence, Taurus and Libra (Venus), and Gemini and Virgo (Mercury).

Saturni sub eo decurrentis, et loco Mercurii
sub praemissa ponitur Mars, sub ♒ Sol,
Mercurius excandens, et retrorsus cedens, sub
♓ Iupiter, et Venus et Luna cum eo. cum malignis
Cauda, vel cum Luna.
IMAGO ♎ facta secundum artem, valida est
multiplicans, et confortans humanam naturam, et item
cetera animantium genera, maiores aves. specialiter autem perutilis est his quos gubernat
signum, quorum videlicet fuerit horoscopans,
aut annuae conversionis, vel cum ad eum pervenit
motrix ex directione, aut profectione ab aliquo
hilegiorum. Sapientes quoque, theologos, et quorum
est exercitium circa res divinas. Rursus autem
vigorat, et in sanitate custodit membra omnia
quae signum gubernat, et ab eorum aegritudinibus
praeservat, et factis est adiutorium curae. Sunt
haec stomachi partes inferae, et ancharum loca, et
adiacentia membra. fertiles quoque facit agros, et

of Saturn traveling under it, and
Mars having been placed in the house of Mercury. The Sun shall be
    under Aquarius,
Mercury combust and moving retrograde.
Jupiter shall be under Pisces, and Venus and the Moon together with
    it. Cauda Draconis shall be with the malefics, or with the Moon.
THE IMAGE OF LIBRA made according to the art is good for
augmenting and strengthening the human nature, and likewise
other types of creatures, moreso the birds,
but it is specifically very useful for those whom the sign governs,
namely those for whom it is ascending,
or (governs) according to their annual (solar) return, or when
(an influence) reaches the sign from someone's hyleg by direction or
    profection.
Also the wise, theologians, and those whose
occupation concerns divine things. And it also
invigorates and keeps sound all the (bodily) members
which the sign governs, and protects them from their illnesses,
and is an aid in effecting a cure: these are
the lower parts of the stomach, and the hips, and
adjacent members. It makes fields and meadows fertile as well,

Divinum Opus de Magia Disciplina

prata, atque segetes multiplicat, est enim sub
ea imago spicae, haec gubernans terras, et loca
quorum est signum gubernator, sive natura, sive
accidenti. excitat item essentiales qualitates colorem
cum humorem, proprea multis passionibus utilis
esse prohibetur. partes item quas signum gubernat,
admovet ventos, et demones adducit, et
universaliter vigorat omnia accidentia, et res gubernationis
signi. Hora quidem compositionis eius est, quotiens gradus
.13. horoscopat, sub quo in praesenti pervenit
ad exortum, stella imaginis Spicae, primam sortita
magnitudinem, et sub ea ♀ decurrat, et ☽
cum ea. Sol autem, et ♂ sub ♏. Sub ♐ ♄,
his exagonas. fit etenim utilis proprie amicabilitatem
eius ad horoscopans signum sub quo est eius honor,
cadant ♂ et ☋. Imprimitur autem, vel infunditur
imago, qualis in orbe stellato pingitur signis.
et dicunt qui sit forma viri erecti stantis, altera manu tenentis bilances aequatas, super

[10r]

and also multiplies crops, for under
this sign is the image of Spica, this star managing lands and places
of which the sign is governor, whether by nature or
accident. Likewise it excites the essential qualities of hotness[38]
and wetness—particularly the many passions that it is useful
to restrain—and it rouses the winds and attracts the demons of those
    sorts which the sign governs, and in general invigorates all the
    accidents and things governed by
the sign. In any case, the time of its composition is when the
thirteenth degree (of Libra) rises—under which at present
the first-magnitude star of the image, Spica,[39] appears at dawn—
and Venus travels under this sign, and the Moon
together with it. And the Sun and Mars are under Scorpio; Saturn
    shall be under Capricorn,
sextile to them—for it becomes particularly useful to propitious ends
at the rising of the sign under which is its exaltation.[40]
Mars and Cauda Draconis shall be cadent. And the image is
    imprinted or cast
as the sign is depicted in the stellar sphere.
And they say that the form shall be that of a man standing upright,
    in one
hand holding balanced scales; above

---

38 Reading, with Plut. 44.35, 203r, *calorem* for *colorem*.

39 As of the year 2023, Spica is at 24°09' ♎. Given sidereal precession of approximately 1° every 72 years, we can calculate that Spica was at 13° ♎ circa 1231, dating Anselmi's astronomical source to almost two centuries prior to the time of his writing in the early 1400s.

40 Saturn is exalted at 21° ♎.

cuius caput est avis, cuius altera medietas alba,
altera nigra. Si tamen intentio fuerit artificis
opus fieri ad segetes, et semina, sufficit figura
spicae, funditur vero ex auro, vel argento, aut
in aliqua ex dictis gemmis. Ad nocendum fit
cum sub adiunctorum loco Mars decurrit. sub
signo ♏ Sol. ambo ♀ ☿ radiis excandescentes,
et retrorsus accedentes. sub ♒ Saturnus re-
motus ab conspectu Martis. Iupiter, Saturno diameter, aut sub Tauro, Luna cum Iove.
☋ cum malignorum altera, vel cum Iove.
IMAGO ♏ est vigorans, confortans et
multiplicans animantia omnia quae signum gubernat.
sunt item quae in aquis degunt serpentes, serpentia,
et reptilia quae terrae cavernas, et fluminum,
et putrida loca inhabitant. homines item quos
gubernat signum quorum fit radix horoscopans,
aut annuae conversionis, vel cum ad eum pervenit
motus per directionem, aut profectionem et quorum

his head is a bird, of which one half is white,
the other black. If, however, the intention of the artificer
is that the work should be for crops and seeds, then the form of
   Spica[41] suffices,
but cast from gold or silver, or
(engraved) in one of the aforementioned gemstones. To cause injury,
   it shall be made
when Mars travels through an adjacent house.
The Sun shall be under the sign of Scorpio, both Venus and Mercury
   burned by its rays
and moving retrograde. Saturn under Aquarius shall be far
from any aspect with Mars. Jupiter and Saturn shall be opposed,
or Jupiter shall be under Taurus, the Moon with Jupiter (in either
   case).
Cauda Draconis shall be with one of the malefics, or with Jupiter.
THE IMAGE OF SCORPIO invigorates, strengthens, and
multiplies all creatures which the sign governs,
serpents which live in the water as well as serpents
and reptiles which inhabit caverns and riversides
and putrid places on land. Likewise people whom
the sign governs, for whom it is in the ascendant natally,
or (governs) according to their annual (solar) return, or when
(an influence) reaches it by direction or profection, and those whose

---

41 "Spica" is literally the word for an ear of grain.

est exercitium in fusione sanguinis, et me-
dicandi. et hic quidem proprie in conditis corporum partibus quae gubernat, vessica, anus, pu-
denda, et in sanitate conservat, an aegritudinibus
apta praeservat, factas curat. et item in quosdam
communes morbos, et lepra, cancrum faciei,
pustulas, oculorum aegritudines, membrorum fractiones.
augmentum bonum confert arboribus, et plantis
quae in aquis crescunt, et circa ea loca. Rursus
cum signum natale gubernat, et accidentaliter,
confortat, excitat, item, et elementales qualitates,
friges, et humores. has enim signum gubernat, uti
cholericis corporibus, et his qui in cholericas
aegritudines cadunt pro utiles fore creduntur.
Excitat vero partis quam gubernat signum ventos
et movet demones, praecipue malignos, et universaliter res,
et accidentia signi. Est vero compositionis hora, quotiens
sub eius horoscopante loco decurrit Sol, Mars
sub ♏ illi exagonas, vel sub ♌, vel sub ♎,

occupation is bloodletting and medicine,
and this especially pertaining to the private
parts of the body, the bladder, anus,
genitalia, which the sign governs and keeps healthy, readily preserv-
　ing them from illnesses,
effecting cures, and doing likewise for some
common[42] diseases, and leprosy, facial ulcers,
pustules, illnesses of the eyes, (and) broken limbs.
It confers good growth upon trees, and plants
which grow in and around water. Again,
when the sign governs natally, or by accident,
it likewise strengthens (and) excites the elemental qualities
of coldness and wetness, for the sign governs these, as
will be found useful for choleric bodies, and those who
fall into choleric illnesses.
But it summons winds and rouses demons of the sort governed by
　the sign,
especially the malicious ones, and in general the things
and accidents belonging to the sign. But the time of its composition
　is when
the Sun rises under this sign. Mars
under Capricorn shall be sextile to it, or under Leo or Libra.

---

42 Or possibly "communicable".

Mercurius cadens, et recedens retrorsus, cum eo ♀
aut cum ♂, sub ♐ Iupiter, aut sub ♌, proprie
sub eo Mars. Luna cum Iove, aut Mars, Saturnus
a Marte cadat, et ab horoscopo. Quidam haec
imaginis componendam scripserunt, quotiens ☽ sub hoc
signo decurrit horoscopans, et de Sole diximus,
aut aliquem cardinem tenens. et laudant ad morsus
sive puncturas scorpionum, est vero validior in
bezaar lapillo sculpta. hoc quidem sigillo thus,
aut mastiche, vel simile retinens figuram
sigilletur, et exhibeatur percusso in potu, sine mora
liberabitor. Est vero imaginis figura qualis in orbe
pingitur. Siquidem ad nocendum fit, decurrat
sub ea Saturnus, et Venus, aut Luna. ☿ quoque
retrorsus incedat, sub ♌ illi tetragonus. sub ☉
Sol trigonus. cadant ♃, et ♂, ab eo. cum ipso ☋,
vel cum ☽. Fundatur ex plumbo, vel figuretur
in aliquo ex nominatus lapillis qui malignarum
sectantur motus. Adgregant haec imago

GIORGIO ANSELMI/Brian Johnson

Mercury shall be cadent and moving retrograde. Venus shall be with Mercury
or with Mars. Jupiter shall be under Sagittarius, or under Leo—especially if
Mars is in that sign. The Moon shall be with Jupiter or Mars. Saturn shall be
cadent from Mars and from the ascendant. Some
have written that this image shall be composed when the Moon rises under
this sign, just as we have said regarding the Sun,
or occupies a cardinal (house), and they laud (its efficacy) against the bite
or sting of the scorpion. But it is stronger if
sculpted in a bezoar stone, (and) indeed frankincense,
or mastic, or a similar (substance) capable of retaining the shape is stamped with this figure,
and it is administered by putting it in a drink; without delay
(the patient) will be delivered. But the form of the image is as depicted in the (celestial) sphere.
And if it is to cause injury,
Saturn shall be under this sign, together with Venus or the Moon. And Mercury shall be
moving retrograde under Leo, squaring Saturn.
The Sun under Cancer shall be trine Saturn. Jupiter and Mars shall be cadent from it. Cauda Draconis shall be with (it),[43]
or with the Moon. It is cast from lead, or sculpted
in one of the aforementioned stones which
follow the movement of the malign (stars). This image attracts

---

43 The syntax of this passage is very ambiguous, and the celestial body from which Jupiter and Mars are cadent, and with which Cauda Draconis is located, may be either the Sun or Saturn.

malignae naturae animantia venenosa, serpentina, et
nocentia facit, praeter modum nocens, omnibus
insuper quibus utiles fore praediximus, excitat res,
et accidentia, adversa.
IMAGO ♐ potens est, et valida,
confortans humanam speciem, animantia grossa, subiugalia, et equitabilia, speciem quidem equinam. specialiter vero homines quos signum gubernat, quorum
radix fuerit horoscopans, vel annuae conversionis,
sicut in praemissis. Rursus autem exaltat, et magnificat reges, et nobiles, et potentes, exaltatque
sterpe progenitos ordinis equestris, et item legis
peritos, et hos a nocivis praeservat eventibus.
morsus item bestiarum vetat, et casus ex illis,
ab oculorum damnamentis praeservat, et exauget
mineras, et generaliter omnia loca quae subsunt gu-
bernationi signi vigorat qualitates, excitat
calidum, et siccum praeservans, praeter haec corpora
abundantia superfluo flegmate, et ab aegritudinibus

GIORGIO ANSELMI / Brian Johnson

[12r]

venomous creatures of a malign nature, serpents, and
causes injury. Besides its harmful manner, in everything
preceding in which we have said the image will be useful, this one sets in motion things
and accidents to the contrary.
THE IMAGE OF SAGITTARIUS is powerful and capable
in strengthening the human form; creatures that are large, put under the yoke,
and fit for riding, at least the equine species;
but especially those people whom the sign governs, for whom
it is in the ascendant natally, or (governs) according to their annual (solar) return,
just as in the preceding. And moreover it exalts and glorifies
kings, and nobles, and potentates, and it elevates
the progeny of the knightly class, and likewise those skilled in law,
and it protects them from harmful events.
Likewise it prevents beasts from biting, and accidents involving them.
It protects the eyes from injury, and increases (the yield of)
mines, and in general it invigorates the qualities of all places that are governed
by the sign, exciting
hotness and dryness. Moreover it protects bodies
from an overabundance of phlegm, and cures them of illnesses

praeter haec curans, et proprie corpora haec tempore
hyemis vigorat. Ventos partis quam gubernat signum excitat, et demones proprie adducit, et
universaliter movet res, et accidentia gubernationis signi.
Est autem compositionis hora quotiens Sol sub haec
decurrens signa horoscopat. sub signo ♓ Iupiter
tetragonus, aut sub ♈ trigonus. Luna cum eo. sub
♎ Venus. cum Sole Mercurius. malignae cadant
utraque cum ♉. aut sub ♏ Mars. aut Iovi
adiunctus. aut sub ♒ Iupiter, et Saturnus Soli
tetragoni. Fundatur ex auro, vel argento, aut
sculpatur in aliqua ex gemmis, quae harum stellarum
sectantur motus. est vero figura imaginis imprimenda
qualis in stellato orbe pingitur. ponitur vero hominis
arcu sagittantis imago, cuius est inferior ab umbilico
pars equina. Quidam figurant hominem
curti, et torti colli, in cuius dexter est avis. Ad
nocendum vero, Saturnus sub hoc signo decurrat
horoscopans, illi Mars adiunctus, aut diameter,

besides, and particularly invigorates bodies in the winter time.
It rouses winds and attracts demons of the sort which the sign governs, and
in general moves things and accidents governed by the sign.
And the time of its composition is when the Sun
rises under this sign; Jupiter under the sign of Pisces shall be squaring it,
or under Aries forming a trine to the Sun. The Moon shall be together with (Jupiter).
Venus shall be under Libra, Mercury with the Sun. Both the malefics shall be
cadent, together with Cauda Draconis; or, Mars shall be under Capricorn or
conjunct Jupiter; or, Jupiter shall be under Aquarius, and Saturn shall square the Sun.
It is cast from gold or silver, or
sculpted in one of the gemstones which follow the movement of these stars,
but the form of the image is imprinted
as depicted in the stellar sphere. Indeed, the image is fashioned (in the likeness) of a man
shooting arrows with a bow, of whom the part below the abdomen is
like a horse. (However,) some make the figure of a short man,
with a twisted neck, in whose right hand is a bird.
But to cause injury, Saturn shall be rising under this sign,
Mars conjoining it, or in opposition,

Divinum Opus de Magia Disciplina

aut tetragonus, Sol item sit illi diameter, et ☿
et Venus cum eis, vel sub ♋, ☊ cum ☽, vel
cum malignarum altera.
IMAGO ♑ confortat, et vigorat, et
multiplicat animantia quadrupedia, quae tamen
non sint subiugo ponenda, aut equitatu exer-
cenda, sed minuta, cornuta, domestica,
caprae, oves, et similia. Rursus autem homines
confortat quorum gubernator est signum, secundum
modos quos exposuimus. rursus autem populares
et rusticos, et infime conditionis. partes vero
corporis quas signum gubernat iuncturas, crura,
conservat sana, et aegritudines factas curae,
et ab oculorum aegritudine praeservat, et lepra,
et a ceteris cutis defedationibus, et universaliter a morbis
melancholicis. loca rursus omnia quae signum
gubernat, salvat sive naturas, sive accidenti.
Semina item, et terras cultas. admovet item
in aere qualitates gubernati elementi, frigus

GIORGIO ANSELMI / Brian Johnson

or square. The Sun shall likewise be in opposition to it, and Mercury
and Venus with them,[44] or under Cancer. Cauda Draconis shall be
 with the Moon, or
with one of the malefics.
THE IMAGE OF CAPRICORN strengthens and invigorates and
multiplies four-footed creatures, but not those
put under the yoke, or used for riding,
but the small, horned, domesticated ones,
goats, sheep, and the like. On the other hand, it also strengthens
 those people
whom the sign governs, after
the manner I have explained, and also common people
and rustics, and those of the lowest status. And indeed it keeps
 healthy the parts
of the body which the sign governs, the joints, the legs,
and effects the cures of illnesses,
and protects against illness of the eyes, and leprosy,
and other corruptions of the skin, and in general melancholic
 diseases.
And again, it secures all the places which the sign
governs, whether by nature or accident,
likewise seeds and cultivated lands. And it brings
to the air those elemental qualities it governs, coldness

---

44 The plural pronoun here presumably refers to the Sun and Mars, but the text is ambiguous.

cum sicco quibus imago fit pro utilis, aerem removens
pestiferum, et illi prorsus repugnans pro corruptiones.
ventos partis signi, et demones advocat: Universaliter
autem admovet res, et accidentia gubernationis signi.
Est vero tempus compositionis, quotiens sub eo decurrens
Sol horoscopat, sub ♎ Saturnus, aut sub ♓ cum
Iove. sub ♏ Mars, Soli exagonus, aut sub ♈
tetragonus. cum ♃ Venus, et ☽. cadant ☿ et ☋.
funditur ex auro, vel argento, aut imprimitur
in aliqua ex dictis gemmis. figura vero qualis
pingitur in orbe stellato, quidam figuram
dicunt haeduli albi, cuius est ventris medietas
nigra. vel sub eo decurrat Saturnus, foelix
similiter, et Mars luminaribus trigoni, vel exagoni.
Ad nocendum decurrat Sol, et ☽, et ☋, sub eo. sub
♏ ♃, aut sub ♎. ♂ et ♄ sub ♌. sub
♏, ♀, et ☿ cum Sole. formetur imago ex ferro,
vel fundatur ex plumbo, aut sculpatur in quidam ex gemmis, quae
malignarum motus sectari reditus est.

and dryness, whereby the image is made useful, removing pestilential air,
and utterly resisting corruptions to it.
It summons winds and demons of the sort belonging to the sign,
and in general it attracts the things and accidents governed by the sign.
But the time of its composition is when
the Sun rises under this sign. Saturn shall be under Libra, or under Pisces with
Jupiter. Mars under Scorpio shall be sextile the Sun, or under Aries
and squaring the Sun. Venus and the Moon shall be with Jupiter.
Mercury and Cauda Draconis shall be cadent.
It is cast from gold or silver, or engraved
in one of the aforementioned gemstones, but the figure is as
depicted in the stellar sphere: some say the figure
of a white kid, half[45] of whose belly is
black. Or, (it may be made when) Saturn travels under the sign, similarly fortunate,
and Mars is trine or sextile the luminaries.
To cause injury, the Sun and Moon and Cauda Draconis shall be traveling under this sign.
Jupiter shall be under Scorpio or Libra, Mars and Saturn under Leo,
Venus under Scorpio, and Mercury with the Sun. The image is formed from iron,
or cast from lead, or sculpted in one of the gemstones which
follow the revolutions of the malign (stars).

---

45 Or, "the middle".

IMAGO ♒ MOVET UNIVERSALITER, ET ADDUCIT
res, et accidentia quae signum gubernat, vigorat, et
confortat, quotiens fiet hora quam dicemus,
specialiter quidem humanam speciem, et inter homines praecipue quos signi gubernat, sive ex radice
sive alter, ut in ceteris praedictus est. omnes rursus
quorum est exercitium in aquis, et circa eas. Sapientes
item et doctos inter homines. corpora vero humana in
sanitate conservat, et ab aegritudinibus, et morbis praeservat, factus curat, praecipue morbos
mulierum, et amplius in omnibus quae signum
gubernat. confortat insuper et aerem bonum facit,
et reliqua in terris, et locis quae signum sive natura,
sive accidenti gubernat, maria, flumina,
decursus aquarum, et quorum aedificia sunt in eis.
Calorem inter elementales qualitates excitat cum
humore. hinc corpora melancholica adiuvat
et vigorat. praeservat aptos in eas aegritudines
cadere, provocat signi gubernationis ventos

GIORGIO ANSELMI / Brian Johnson

[14r]

In general, the IMAGE OF AQUARIUS moves and attracts
the things and accidents which the sign governs, invigorates, and
strengthens, when it is made at the time which we will declare,
especially the human species, and among them chiefly
those governed by the sign, either natally
or otherwise, as has been said regarding the others, but also all
whose occupation is in and around the water, and the wise
and learned among people likewise. Indeed, it keeps the human body
healthy, and preserves it from illnesses and diseases,
effecting the cure thereof—especially illnesses
of women—and moreover it strengthens everything which the sign
governs. It makes the air pleasant as well,
and likewise so in the lands and places which the sign governs, whether by nature
or accident—seas, rivers,
the course of waters—and those buildings that are in them.
Among the elemental qualities, it excites hotness and
wetness, so it cheers and invigorates melancholic bodies,
bound to which it protects from falling ill.
It provokes the winds and demons governed by the sign.

Divinum Opus de Magia Disciplina

et demones. Est autem compositionis ipsius hora quotiens
Saturnus exortu matutino Solem noviter
eo sub signo praecesserit, et sub ♓ decurrat
Sol. Sub ♐ ♃, Saturno exagonus. Mercurius
et Venus cum Sole. sub ♈ ☽. cadant ♂ et ☋.
Figura est qualis pingitur in orbe signorum. funditur
ex auro, aut argento, vel imprimitur gemmae
utili ex antedictis. Est autem figura hominis tenentis
urnam, effundentis ex ea aquarum multitudinem.
Ad nocendum fit cum Sol sub eo decurrit, sub
♉ Mars, tetragonus illi. Venus et ☽ sub ♐, vel ♑.
cum Sole ♃, aut ☋. cadant ☽ cum ☋, vel ☋
cum Sole.
IMAGO ♓ confortat animantia praecipue
aquatilia, pisces, ostracosa, et aves circa aquas
degentes, et homines, praesertim quos signum gubernat,
sicut in praemissis expositus est, et item quorum est
exercitium, et opus circa aquas, et circa res aquatiles.
Sanas custodit corporis partes quas signum gubernat

And the time of its composition is when
Saturn first appears in this sign before sunrise,
and the Sun travels under Pisces.
Jupiter under Sagittarius shall be sextile Saturn. Mercury
and Venus shall be with the Sun. The Moon shall be under Ares.
    Mars and Cauda Draconis shall be cadent.
The figure is as depicted in the sphere of the signs, cast
from gold or silver, or engraved in
one of the aforementioned suitable gemstones. And it is the figure of
    a person holding
an urn, pouring from it a multitude of waters.
To cause injury it is made when the Sun travels under this sign,
Mars under Taurus squaring it. Venus and the Moon shall be under
    Sagittarius or Capricorn.
Jupiter shall be with the Sun or with Cauda Draconis. The Moon
    shall be cadent with Cauda Draconis, or Cauda Draconis
shall be with the Sun.
THE IMAGE OF PISCES chiefly strengthens
aquatic creatures, fish, crustaceans, and birds living around the
    water;
also people, particularly those the sign governs,
just as explained in the preceding, and likewise those whose
occupation and work is around the water, and concerns aquatic
    things.
It keeps healthy the parts of the body which the sign governs,

et ab eorum aegritudinibus curat, et omne corpus
a cuncti cutaneis defedationibus, a spasmo,
et a nervorum aegritudinibus curat. loca insuper
omnia quae signum gubernat natura, vel accidenti,
custodit, et aere in eis bonum efficit. In am-
mantium corpore, et aere, locorumque quae signum gubernat, movet frigus cum humore.
ideoque perutilis est figura aestate corpora praeservat
cholerica, ne cadant, lapsaque curat a similibus morbis. provocat ventos, et demones
partis mundi quam signum gubernat. Est vero
compositionis tempus, quotiens sub eo decurrens
♃ horoscopat. sub ♈ Sol, aut sub ♉ Iovi exagonus.
Luna cum ♃, aut cum ♀, vel sub ♋, Iovi
trigona. cum Sole ☿. malignae cadant, et ☋.
Figura est piscium qualis in orbe figatur. funditur
autem ex auro, vel argento, vel stagno, aut imprimit chalcedonio, vel topatio, aut simili
gemmae. Ad nocendum fit cum Sol sub eo

and cures them of illnesses, and (cures) the body as a whole
of corruptions of the skin, of spasms,
and of illnesses of the nerves.[46] Furthermore
it preserves all the places which the sign governs by nature or accident,
and makes the air in them pleasant. In its affinity
for the body, and air, and places which the sign
governs, it moves coldness and wetness,
and so the figure is very useful for preserving choleric bodies during the summer,
so they do not pass out or faint, (and) it cures similar
diseases. It provokes the winds and demons
of those parts of the world which the sign governs. But
the time of its composition is when Jupiter rises under this sign.
The Sun shall be under Aries, or under Taurus sextile Jupiter.
The Moon shall be with Jupiter or with Venus, or under Cancer
trine Jupiter. Mercury shall be with the Sun. The malefics and Cauda Draconis shall be cadent.
The figure is of fishes, as fixed in the (celestial) sphere,
and cast from gold, or silver, or tin, or engraved
in chalcedony, or topaz, or a similar
gemstone. To cause injury, it is made when the Sun travels under this sign,

---

46 Or of the muscles, or tendons.

decurrit, et ♄ sub ♐ Soli tetragonus. sub ♈
Iupiter, Venus cum eo. ☽ cum ☿ vel ♄, et Cauda.
funditur autem, vel imprimatur sicut qualiter dicta sunt ad
    nocendum.

Notificatio modorum componendi images boreales
octavi orbis ultra zodiacum. Capitulum .2^{m}.

Est monstratum in universalibus, qui ultra
zodiacum cuius est latitudo gradu .6. in parte
utramque, pinguntur rursus images .21. boreali
ex parte, et sunt nominate, et figurate nominibus,
et rebus assimilate, quas in hoc mundo inferior
gubernant, et quas admovet motrices sub
illis ambulantes, relate tamen ad hymeri
circuli loca quae tenent in radice, secundum rationem
quam in .12. signis praediximus. Unde fit cum
imago ursae dicta sit, quia eius est gubernare
animalia sylvestra, et praecipue speciei huius, et
motrix quotiens fuerit sub ea fortis, et foelix superiorum animantium individua multiplicare,
et vigorare. Contra cum fuerit maligna motrix

and Saturn under Sagittarius squares the Sun.
Venus shall be with Jupiter under Ares. The Moon and Cauda Draconis shall be with Mercury or Saturn.
And it is cast or imprinted in just the same way as the aforementioned (images) for causing injury.

CHAPTER TWO: *A Note on the Methods of Composing the Images of the Eighth Sphere That Lie North of the Zodiac.*

It is generally demonstrated that outside
the Zodiac, of which the latitude is six degrees
on each side, there are also images depicted, twenty-one on the northern
side, and they are named, and have figures according to their names.
And they are assimilated to the things which they govern in this lower world,
and which the motive (stars)
traveling under them conduct, yet (those stars) relate to the places of the *hymeri*[47]
circle which they occupy in the root, according to the manner
which we spoke of in reference to the twelve signs. Whence, in the case of
the image called the Bear—because it governs
the animals of the forest, and especially that species—
when the motive (star) under this image is strong and fortunate,
members of the higher creatures are multiplied and invigorated.

---

47 Or *hymen*, as per Plut. 44.35; in both cases, the final letters are written with a superscript notation indicating a contraction. I have been unable to identify the intended term, and the meaning of this passage remains obscure.

et infoelix, damnare hac eadem ratione, et in
magnis. serpentes gubernare, et reptilia. et
motrici sub ea decurrenti, si benigna est fortis, et foelix, multiplicare, congregare, con-
fortare, et movere. Contra maligne. Sic
secundum eandem rationem se habent res de imaginibus
ceteris, quae unaquaeque gubernet res similes
in his horis debitae impressae moveant, et regulent
res, et accidentia, proprea quae adiunctae sunt motrices, et gubernatrices. et erit motus secundum
qualitates traditam imagini in radice. fortassis tamen fiet res, et accidens manifestus per
amplius et in animantibus, et brutis quam in homines.
cum sit homo animal utens ratione, et discursu hu-
manis legibus dispositus, atque divinis. et
his reguletur, vivat, et doctrinetur, quamvis itaque
perveniat ad imaginem accidentis motrices, et ex-
citet eius voluntatem imaginis vis, et proprietas
sua fortitudine, non tamen ostentabitur in eo accidens

GIORGIO ANSELMI / Brian Johnson

On the contrary, when the motive (star) is malign
and infortunate, the image condemns them by this same reasoning, and
greatly so—(instead) it governs serpents and reptiles. And
if the motive (star) traveling under this image is benign,
strong, and fortunate, (it acts to) multiply, gather, strengthen,
and move (creatures); to the contrary if it is malign. Thus
by the same reasoning the other images preside over things,
each of them governing things similar to them
at those times at which they must be imprinted, moving and regulating
things and accidents, particularly those (images) which are joined to the motive (stars)
and lords, and the movement shall be according to
the qualities bestowed upon the image according to the root.
But it may be that a thing or accident will manifest
moreso in animals and brutes than in humans,
because a human is an animal that uses reason, and its behavior
is disposed according to human and divine laws, and
it is ruled, maintained, and directed by these, so that although
it may happen upon an image (bearing) the accidents of the motive (stars), and
the power and properties of the image rouse its will
by force, nonetheless (that human) will not exhibit the accident which the image motivates.

Divinum Opus de Magia Disciplina

quid motura est imago. Animantia vero quae
sub hominis regulatione reguntur, et teneatur, et
si cum perveniant ad locum imaginis excitentur, harum
tamen regulator homine impellit forte fortius excitans quam
spiritualis possit vis imaginis. Libera vero animantia
quae neque lege cohercita, neque ratione, neque
verecundia moventur, neque doctrinis regulata
sunt, quibus natalis solus instinctus praedominatur, et
gubernat imago super celestis. et admovet
sub ea decurrens stella, et facta imago pariter,
nisi quaestum prohibet locus in quo sita
fuerit. Sunt in quibus apparet accidentis
motus. Non siquidem egredientur serpentes ad forum
ubi aggregans imago foret sepulta, neque ferae
sylvestres, aut aves his publicis congregarent
in locis ulla vis imaginis. Cum tamen fuerit reposita in locis conversationis earum apparet perfecto
motus accidentis quod fuerit motura imago
veluti si fuerit imago ad congregandum columbas,

GIORGIO ANSELMI / Brian Johnson

Indeed, creatures that
are ruled and bound by human governance,
if they come to a place to which an image attracts them, nonetheless
may be roused more powerfully by the commands of the human
 driving them than
by the spiritual power of the image. But free creatures
which are neither coerced by law, nor reason, nor
moved by shame, nor governed by teachings,
in which the native instinct alone predominates, and
which a supercelestial image governs, and
a star traveling beneath it conducts, and (for which) an image is
 made likewise—
unless the place in which it would be located prohibits the use
 (thereof)—
such are those in which a motivated accident appears.
Hence serpents will not be brought into a busy marketplace
should an image be buried there, nor will beasts
of the forest or birds congregate in such public places
by the power of any image. But when it is hidden
in their familiar place, it appears to bring about
the accidental movement which the image sets in motion—
if, for instance, there were an image to make doves flock together,

movebuntur ad turrim in qua sita fuerit imago.
Quae saltem in horizonte quodam visa fuerit. et praecipue ex ea parte unde fuerit situs, et conspe-
ctus, aut saltem ex locis unde possit turris
videri. Animantia itaque quae sub hominis custodia
sunt, et vinculis tenentur, et fuste moventur. Item
neque homines verecundi, aut lege, vel doctrina
vel ratione utuntur, appetitu, et inclinationem
praedominante non moventur. Ideoque cum fiunt
imagines ad accidens movendum, quod contra bonos
mores, contra honestatem, contra leges fiunt
patriae. proprie autem cum in palam movendum fiunt,
pauci, aut nulli motus videbuntur, quales
sunt imagines, quae fiunt ut homines se in publicis
locis denudent, aut sedeant in locis ubi sederit
non convenit, aut cantent ubi cantare non
licet, stoliditas iudicetur, aut amentia.
Quae autem movent accidentia, ita tamen ut in pu-
blico non appareat motus, sed in occulto,

GIORGIO ANSELMI / *Brian Johnson*

[17r]

(and) move to a tower in which the image shall have been set,
which shall at least be visible on the horizon to one of them, and
    especially
from that region whence (the bird) has been let go, and (the tower) is
    seen,
or (the bird) is at least (let go) from a place where the tower can
be seen—creatures, therefore, which are kept by humans,
and held in bondage, and driven by the goad. Likewise,
people who know shame, or who make use of law, or teaching,
or reason, are unmoved except by appetite and predominant inclina-
    tion. And so, when
images are made to move accidents which are contrary to good
behavior, contrary to honesty, contrary to the laws
of (one's) homeland, but especially when they are (to be) moved
    openly,
little or no movement shall be seen: such as
images fashioned to make people
uncover themselves in public, or sit in places where
it is not fit to sit, or sing where singing is not
allowed (or) is judged stupid or insane.
(With) those, however, that move accidents so that nonetheless
the movement does not appear publicly, but in secret,

magis efficares videntur, veluti si ad amorem
in occulto posita fuerit, haec movet sive virum
sive mulierem ut apparet in occulto alterum
alterius amplexum. Rursus autem imago quae ad
bonos et laudatos promovet mores, non lege
prohibitos, sed honestate commendatos haec. Sunt
ex his quorum sunt potentes motus, veluti
quae ad reconciliationem amicorum sunt, vel fiunt,
et viri et uxoris: et domini et servi. Hic palam
fit quae cum quaerit artifex plenum accidentis
motum ex imagine, quotiens habuerit horam radicis aptam, et fortem, consideret diligenter movendum accidens: et quo loco moveri oportet
ut motum aptam motui accidentis accipiat.
Ponamus itaque proprietates imaginum quae sunt
ex circulum signorum ex eius boreali parte
quae sunt .21. numero, et tempora, et figurationes.
Est vero inter eas apud polum dictum
IMAGO URSAE MAIORIS, huius est gubernare

GIORGIO ANSELMI / Brian Johnson

great effects are seen—if, for instance,
(an image) for love is secretly placed, moving either a man
or a woman to arrive in secret, one
to be embraced by the other. Conversely, an image which
promotes good and laudable behaviors,
which are not prohibited by law, but commended with honor—
powerful impulses come from these, such as
images which are (placed), or made, for the reconciliation of friends,
and of men and wives, and masters and servants. This is plainly
what occurs when an artificer seeks to move an accident completely
by means of an image, so long as a strong and appropriate time to
    begin is at hand, considering carefully
the accident to be moved, and in what place it is opportune for it to
    be moved
so that it receives a movement proper to moving that accident.
Therefore we shall set down the properties of the images that are
outside the circle of the signs, those of the northern part,
which are twenty-one in number, and their times and formations.
Indeed, among them is the image near the pole called
THE GREAT BEAR, which governs

Divinum Opus de Magia Disciplina

sylvestria maiora ex animantibus, et feris.
Cui similis est ursae minoris imago.
Hora quidem imprimendi est, quotiens sub ea
Sol decurrit, aut ☽ sub stellis earum quae ad
ortum perveniunt, et 2.^{am} sortitae sunt magnitudinem
inter quas est quae hyliage, vel halyoze dicitur,
potens. et si Sol subambulet, ☽ sit illi trigona, vel
exagona, et Lunae Venus eadem aspecta con-
iuncta. cum Sole Mercurius, aut cum ☽, aut
cum Venere. malignae cadant, et ☋. Imaginis
huius vis est, feras placidas reddere, mansuetas
et domesticabiles: et earum incursus prohibere.
Imprimitur autem in aliqua ex gemmis, quae motus
sectantur benignarum, aut funditur ex auro vel argento.
Tertia imago est serpentis qui per has
inter utrasque divitit. haec ab morsu vene-
nosorum praecipue serpentum, et reptilium liberat,
si modo ex ea thus, vel mastiche, aut simile,
masticatum bibatur. prohibet item occursus

GIORGIO ANSELMI / Brian Johnson

the larger woodland creatures and beasts.
THE IMAGE OF THE LITTLE BEAR is similar.
The time at which it is to be imprinted is when
the Sun travels under this image, or the Moon is under
its second-magnitude stars as they are rising,
among which that called Hyliage or Halyoz is
powerful. And if the Sun travels under (this image) the Moon shall
    be trine or sextile to it,
and Venus aspecting the Moon likewise.
Mercury shall be together with the Sun or the Moon or
Venus. The Malefics and Cauda Draconis shall be cadent.
The power of this image is to render beasts peaceful, tame,
and domesticable, and to prevent them from attacking.
And it is engraved in one of the gemstones that
follow the movement of the benign (stars), or cast from gold or
    silver.
THE THIRD IMAGE IS OF A SERPENT[48] which
separates these two.[49] It delivers one from the bite of venomous
creatures, especially serpents and reptiles,
if one simply imbibes frankincense, or mastic, or a similar
gum (fashioned) into its form. Likewise it forbids serpents from
    coming near

---

48 The constellation Draco.
49 I.e., Ursa Major and Minor.

serpentum eius praesentia quantumlibet malignorum
et cogit ne ad eius praesentiam moveantur, sed quiescunt
ut non moveri possint se. Et dicunt quod si fuerint hae .3. imagines simul sculptae, aut separatim
secundum qui in orbe pinguntur, in quadam ex gemmis quae
motum sequntur benignarum, redunt hominem gestante
eas, astutum, fortem, magnanimum, et in proposito
manentem, deo, et hominibus placentem. imprimit autem
in aliqua ex nominatis gemmis, et est praecipua
dragos, aut bezaar, aut funditur in auro, aut argento.
QUARTA IMAGO quae nominatur a phtolomaeus
INFLAMMATUM. huius est vis ad excitandum febres,
aut etiam ad inducendum demones eius in corpus, pro
quo facta fuerit, sive sculpta. Est autem hora
quotiens Saturnus, aut Mars horoscopat, hac
imagine horoscopante, et sint illis diametra
luminaria ambo, vel tetragona. Iupiter cadant, et
sit ☋ cum malignarum altera, aut cum Luna.
imprimitur in onichino, aut magnete, vel in

its presence, no matter how vicious,
and compels them not to approach, but to be quiescent,
so that they cannot move themselves. And they say that if
these three images[50] are sculpted together, or separately,
according to what is depicted in the (celestial) sphere, in one of the gemstones which
follow the movement of the benign (stars), they render the person bearing
them cunning, strong, brave, and enduring in their undertakings,
pleasing to men and God. And it is engraved
in one of the aforementioned gemstones, and especially
dragos, or bezoar, or cast from gold or silver.
THE FOURTH IMAGE,[51] called by Ptolemy
"THE INFLAMED ONE",[52] has the power to incite fevers,
or even to send demons thereof into the body, for
which purpose it is fashioned or sculpted. And the time (for doing so) is
when Saturn or Mars rises while this image is ascending,
and both luminaries are opposing or squaring them. Jupiter shall be cadent, and
Cauda Draconis with one of the malefics, or with the Moon.
It is engraved in onyx or lodestone, or in

---

50 Presumably Draco, Ursa Major, and Ursa Minor.
51 The constellation Cepheus.
52 From the Arabic *al-Multaheb*.

Divinum Opus de Magia Disciplina

gihagaha, vel simili, aut funditur in ferro, vel plumbo.
Quinta imago est ululantis, sive voci
ferantis imago. haec gestantem facit potentem
supra demones et eius vocationi advenientes, et con-
stringere eos, et respondere. Est autem eius figura
viri cuius in manu altera est diabolus, altera
serpentem tenet, et super eius humeros sunt
ambo sol, et luna, sub pedibus eius leonem con-
culcat. imprimitur autem in diacodo, et ligatur in
plumbo, et secundum magorum intentionem sub eo
ponitur parum arthemisiae, et fenu greci.
Sexta est Corona borealis. haec est potens gestantem reddere honorandum, famandum,
exaltandum, et magnificandum, et laudandum, et gratum
fieri regibus, et principibus. Est autem impressionis
tempus, quotiens cum eius stellis horoscopantibus Sol ad exortum pervenit, et cum Iupiter exortu prevenit
matutino, et ☽ cum eo. cadant malignae cum ☋.
imprimitur autem in onichio, aut funditur ex auro.

gihagaha[53] or the like, or cast from iron or lead.
THE FIFTH IMAGE[54] IS "THE HOWLER",[55] or
an image given to the voice of a wild beast. Bearing this makes one powerful
over demons, and in calling them to come
and respond, and binding them. And its figure
is that of a man holding a devil in one hand,
a serpent in the other, and upon his shoulders are
both the Sun and Moon; he tramples a lion under his feet.
And it is engraved in *diadochos*,[56] and set in
lead, and according to the opinion of the magi,
a bit of artemisia and fenugreek is placed under it.[57]
SIXTH IS THE NORTHERN CROWN.[58] Bearing this has
the power to render one honored, famous,
exalted, and esteemed, and lauded and welcomed
by kings and princes. And the time of its impression is
when the Sun rises with the stars of this image,
and when Jupiter precedes their rising
at dawn, and the Moon is with it. The malefics shall be cadent together with Cauda Draconis.
And it is engraved in onyx, or cast from gold.

---

53 While I have not been able to conclusively identify the substance indicated by this term, I suspect the word may be a corruption of *gagates*, from the Greek γαγάτης, referring to jet, a gemstone-quality lignite. The black color of this stone would also place it in accord with the qualities typically exhibited by the other minerals prescribed in this passage, onyx and lodestone; compare *gihazaha* at 28r, below.
54 The constellation Boötes.
55 From the Arabic *al-'Awwa'*.
56 Read for Anselmi's *diacodo*. Diadochos is a (possibly fictitious) stone said to resemble beryl; see Pliny, *Natural History* 37.57.
57 This image and its preparation and use, though not its celestial correlate, are virtually identical to those adduced by Camillo Leonardi in his 1502 *Speculum Lapidum* from the books of Chael and Solomon; see Fiorello, trans., 2022: 42, 51.
58 *Corona Borealis*.

Divinum Opus de Magia Disciplina

Septima imago est incurvati super genua
hanc nominat phtolomaeus Saltatorem, alii Hercules, sive
Genuflexus. haec singulari fit praesidio in
certamine gestanti, et magis pedestri, audacem
facit, fortem, timendum, liberat a periculis, et ferarum indomitarum prohibet incursus. Impressio etiam
est cum Sol horoscopat cum stellis huius imaginis, et fuerit
Mars Solem ortu preveniens, exagonus illi, Iupiter et
Luna idem, vel transferat inter eos Luna trigono,
vel exagono aspectu. Imaginis figura est qualis in orbe
stellarum pingitur, et ut praediximus ea funditur ex
auro, aut imprimitur in adamante vel alectorio, vel similiter.
Octava imago est cadentis vulturis.
Phtolomaeus hanc nominat Testudinem, et Halyoge. huius
est oratori gratus facere, eloquentiam enim dat,
et gratum auditum. dat item amorem mulierum, et
fortunam cum illis. imprimitur autem cum fuerit ambo
☿ ♀ sub hac adiuncti, praecipue autem sub stella
eius primam sortita magnitudinem, quae super eius oculo pingitur,

THE SEVENTH IMAGE IS OF ONE ON BENDED KNEE;
Ptolemy calls this "the dancer",[59] others Hercules, or
"the kneeler". This is made to be carried as an unequaled aid
in battle, and especially for infantry, making them brave,
strong, fearsome, delivering them from dangers, and
preventing the attacks of beasts. And the impression
is made when the Sun rises with the stars of this image. And
Mars shall precede the Sun in rising, sextile to it; Jupiter and
the Moon shall do likewise, or the Moon shall translate light[60] be-
    tween (the Sun and Jupiter) by a trine
or sextile aspect. The form of the image is as depicted in the stellar
    sphere,
and, like I have said before, it is cast from
gold, or engraved in diamond or *alectoria*, or similar.
THE EIGHTH IMAGE IS OF A FALLING VULTURE;
Ptolemy calls this "the lyre",[61] and Halyoge. It
makes an orator pleasing, for it grants eloquence,
and an agreeable audience; likewise it grants the love of women, and
good luck with them. And it is imprinted when both
Mercury and Venus are joined under this image, but especially
    under
its first-magnitude star, which is depicted above its eye—

---

59 Arabic *al-Rāqeṣ*.
60 The simultaneous separation from one aspect and application to another; see de Vore, 2002: 424; Lewis, 2003: 689.
61 The constellation Lyra.

et haec eorum alterius hora, et horoscopantibus
eis, aut coelum tenentibus summum, aut xi.^{am} vel
ix.^{am} non tamen retrorsus incedant, aut radiis ex-
candeant Solis. si tamen cum sole fuerint, sint
uniti, ad haec enim potiores fiunt, et ex eis sit Iupiter
trigonus, aut exagonus. sed in re mulierum cavendum est,
etenim amorem publicat.
NONA, EST IMAGO HABENTIS PALMAM DELIBUTAM.
huius figura est sedentis super sedem. hanc dixit phtolomaeus
Cassiopeam. et est figura mulieris sedentis super sedem,
extendentis brachia, et manus in crucem. haec valida
est in confortatione cordis, et totus in sanitate
custodit corpus, offert propterea solatium post
labores, et optatam requies. Et hora impressionis
est, quotiens Sol sub ea decurrit imagine hora sua
horoscopans cum eius stellis Iupiter, aut illum praecedens
ortu matutino, sit trigonus, vel exagonus, et cum eo Luna.
Siquidem fuerit cum eis Venus foelix, perutilis fit penitus.
Cadant malignae cum ☋. funditur ex auro,

and this has a different rising time than the others—and they are ascending,
or reaching the midheaven, or the eleventh or
ninth (house); nor yet shall they be moving retrograde, or burned by the rays
of the Sun. If, however, they should be together with the Sun, they should be
united with it, for here they are made more capable.[62] And Jupiter shall be
trine or sextile[63] to them. In matters of women, however, beware, for this image makes love public.
NINTH IS AN IMAGE OF ONE HOLDING AN ANOINTED PALM (FROND),
the figure of whom is sitting upon a chair; Ptolemy calls this
Cassiopeia, and it is the figure of a woman sitting upon a chair,
extending arms and hands in the form of a cross. This is good
for strengthening the heart, and keeping the whole body healthy,
whence it bestows relief
and longed-for rest after hardships. And the time of its imprinting is when the Sun rises under this image,
with Jupiter among its stars; or, (Jupiter) shall rise before them
at dawn, being in a trine or sextile (aspect to them), and the Moon together with it.
And if a fortunate Venus is with them, it is made altogether quite useful.
The malefics and Cauda Draconis shall be cadent. It is cast from gold

---

62 This passage seems to be describing the condition of cazimi.
63 The sextile aspect is only noted in Plut. 44.35, 211r.

vel argento, aut sculpitur in gemmis, ut in chalcedonio
aut in alia similis motus.
DECIMA EST IMAGO PERSEI DEFERENTIS
CAPUT ALGOL. haec se ferentes hostem audacem reddit
et promptus, et timendus: ab inimicis tutatur: victor
facit, et ab invidientibus liberat: et a nocivis
casibus tutatur: et a demonum, et malignorum
incursu, a fulgure praeservat, etiam loca in quibus
fuerit, et a tempestate. Est autem tempus quotiens
Sol hora sua horoscopat cum eius stellis. Luna
lumine aucta. cursu quoque velox; sit illi trigona
vel exagona. Iupiter eum matutino preveniens exortu,
et ex aliis foelix, aut saltem Luna. Sit autem ♂
cum Iove, quotiens ad victoriam fit. At sit ad
demonum fugam, cadat. Cadant item ♄, et ☋.
Imprimitur autem proprie in corallo, aut simili gemmae,
vel funditur ex auro, vel argento.
UNDECIMA EST IMAGO RETINENTIS
HABENAS. hanc quidem nominant Agitatorem. Potens

or silver, or sculpted in a gemstone like chalcedony,
or another of similar movement.
TENTH IS AN IMAGE OF PERSEUS CARRYING
CAPUT ALGOL; he bears this and holds it forth fearsomely before
the bold enemy.
It defends against foes, makes one victorious,
and delivers one from envy. It also protects against accidental injuries,
and against the attack of demons and the wicked.
It protects one from lightning and storms, and also (protects) the places in which
it is set. And the time (of its composition) is when
the Sun, in its hour, rises with the stars of this image. The Moon shall be
increasing in light and also moving swiftly, trine
or sextile the Sun. Jupiter shall rise before the Sun at dawn,
and be made fortunate by the others, or at least by the Moon. Mars, however, shall be
together with Jupiter when the image is made for victory, but if to
expel demons, it shall be cadent. Likewise, Saturn and Cauda Draconis shall be cadent.
And it is properly engraved in coral or a similar gemstone,
or cast from gold or silver.
ELEVENTH IS AN IMAGE OF ONE HOLDING
REINS; indeed, they call this one "the charioteer".[64] It is powerful

---

64 The constellation Auriga.

Divinum Opus de Magia Disciplina

[21r]

ad mercaturam, ad monetas, componendas,
et earum exercitio fortunam dare, et divitias
augere. et dicunt de ea, quod si venator ea
bachulo ligatam exagitat, dum canis leporem
insectatur, aut fera, confugit ad ipsum fera, seu
lapus, neque in eius praesentia nocebunt illi canes.
Imprimatur autem quotiens Sol hora sua cum eis stellis
horoscopat, proprie quidem locus noni orbis sub
quo exortu venit stella imaginis huius quae
primam sortita est magnitudinem, et nominata est
Hyrcus, quae super eius sinistra pingitur spatulam.
et dicunt quod sit ☽ foelix, non adiuncta malignis
sed .6. dominatrici diametra, vel tetragona, et
ipsum quae tempore hoc attingit exortam sub .14.
Arietis, erit signum .6. tenet locum Virginis
et eius dominator Mercuris. Sit autem Mars foelix
ortu matutino Solem preveniens, et exagonus.
est autem sculpenda in ferro, aut fundenda ex auro, vel
imprimenda in lapide aquilae, vel agate, vel simili.

in commerce, for money, making deals,
and bestowing prosperity in the exercise thereof, and increasing
    riches.
And they say that if a hunter
ties the image to a staff and shakes it while a dog is pursuing a hare
or (other) beast, the beast or hare flees toward the image,
nor will the dogs harm the animal in the presence of the image.
And it is imprinted when the Sun, in its hour, rises with the stars of
    this image—
indeed, especially (under) that place in the ninth sphere under
which the first-magnitude star of this image rises, and that is called
Hyrcus,[65] which is depicted above the figure's left shoulder—
and they say that the Moon shall be fortunate, not conjoining the
    malefics,
but opposing or squaring the six lords, and
at the same time rising under the fourteenth degree
of Aries. The sign of Virgo and its lord Mercury shall occupy the
    sixth house. And Mars shall be fortunate,
rising before the Sun at dawn, and sextile to it.
And the image is sculpted in iron, or cast from gold, or
engraved in a dark-colored stone, or agate or similar.

---

65 The star Capella.

Divinum Opus de Magia Disciplina

Duodecima est serpentarius. huius est
figurae animantia venenosa, et eorum morsus
prohibere, occursus, et nocumenta veneni omnis,
sive intra corpus sumptus fuerit, sive extra
applicatus. et similiter reptilium repugnat punctoris.
retinet item, et conservat in amore mutuo
virum et uxorem. Imprimatur autem quotiens sub hoc
imagine decurrit Sol, et cum stellis eius horoscopat
hora sua. sit Venus illi unita cum recto procedit
cursu, sic et mercurius. et inter eos trino
aspectu, vel exagono transferat Luna, aut eorum
lumina calligat Iupiter, Solem ortu matutino prae-
veniens, et foelix ex aliis sit. Item Saturnus
foelix, Soli trigonus, aut exagonus, aut cum Iove. cadant
penitus Mars ♄, et ☋. Funditur ex auro, aut
imprimitur in lapide bezoar, aut in agate, vel simili.
.xiii. hanc phtolemaeus hyscuse, sive hastu
dicit. eius est figura harundinis, hasta ad sa-
giptandum, et ponunt quidam calcare eam cadentem

GIORGIO ANSELMI / Brian Johnson

TWELFTH IS SERPENTARIUS,[66] the figure of which
prevents one from meeting with venomous creatures and their bites,
and all harms done by venom,
whether it has been taken within the body or applied externally,
and likewise it repels the bite of reptiles.
It also preserves man and wife in mutual love.
And it is imprinted when
the Sun, in its hour, rises under the stars of this image.
Venus and Mercury moving direct shall be united with it,
and the Moon shall translate light between them by a trine
or sextile aspect; or
Jupiter, rising before the Sun at dawn, shall collect their light,
and shall be made fortunate by the others. Likewise Saturn
shall be fortunate, trine or sextile the Sun, or together with Jupiter.
Mars, Saturn, and Cauda Draconis shall be entirely cadent. It is cast from gold, or
engraved in bezoar stone, or agate or the like.
THE THIRTEENTH Ptolemy calls HYSCUSE, or "THE SPEAR".[67]
Its figure is that of an arrow, a dart for
shooting, and some posit that the Falling

---

66 The constellation Ophiuchus.
67 The constellation Sagitta.

vulturem pedibus. huius est posse gestanti
dare sagittandi gratiam, et eius praesentia variant
aliorum sagittae, et impediuntur. Est vero tempus
cum Sol sub eius decurrens stellis horoscopat hora
sua, et ponatur, si fuerit possible, unitus illi
Mercurius. Mars autem ortu Solem preveniens
mane intueatur eum trigono vel exagono, aut
veneret. sit Iupiter fortis, ex foelix, et ipse
Soli trigonus, aut exagonus, aut ex altero conspectu
Luna transferat inter eos etiam, et ipsa foelix
et Soli trigona, vel exagona. funditur ex ferro, vel
imprimitur in magnete, vel simili.
XIIII. EST IMAGO AQUILAE. et dicitur vultur
volans. haec se gestanti dignitates, honores,
laudes, divitias, fortunas grandes, exal-
tationes, et regum gratiam promittit, et amissas dignitates et honores veteres perditos reparat.
imprimitur autem quotiens Sol sub eius stellis decurrens
horoscopat hora sua, proprie cum stella eiusdem

Vulture treads upon this with its feet. This image has the power
to give grace to the shooting of arrows when carried, and by its presence
the arrows of others are diverted and impeded. And the time (of its composition) is
when the Sun, in its hour, rises under the stars of this image,
and it is posited that, if possible, Mercury should be united with it.
And Mars shall rise before the Sun
at dawn, aspecting it by a trine or sextile, or
applying thereto. Jupiter shall be strong and fortunate, and
trine or sextile the Sun, or
the Moon may even translate light between them by another aspect, and the Moon itself shall be fortunate
and trine or sextile the Sun. It is cast from iron, or
engraved in lodestone or the like.
THE FOURTEENTH IS AN IMAGE OF AN EAGLE,[68] and it is called "the flying vulture".[69]
Carrying this promises dignities, honors,
praises, riches, great fortunes, exaltations,
and the goodwill of kings, and the recovery of lost dignities
and ruined former honors.
And it is imprinted when the Sun, in its hour, rises under the stars of this image,
especially together with the star of the same

---

68 The constellation Aquila.
69 Arabic al-Naṣr al-Ṭā'er.

nominis quae 2.^{am} sortitam est magnitudinem.
☾ quoque sit illi trigona, vel exagona. Iupiter, et
item Mars, ambo Solem prevenientes maneant
aut inter eos transferentes <Luna>[70] trigone, vel
exagone. malignae cadant, et ☋. Impressio
eius in smaragdo, vel adamante, alectorio
proprie, aut ex auro fusa.
XV. EST IMAGO CADENTIS VULTURIS
huius est vis gestanti conferre facundiam, et gratum
auditum. Imprimitur autem quotiens sub ea ambulat
Sol, et horoscopat cum eis stellis hora sua. Sintque
illi Venus, et Mercurius uniti. Luna, et item Iupiter
illis trigoni, vel exagoni, aut sit loco Solis Luna,
uterque Venus, et mercurius illi exagoni. Iupiter item
eodem conspectu illis, et Lunae commixtus, si foelix
fuerit. malignae cadant, et ☋. funditur ex
auro, vel argento, aut imprimitur alicui
ex gemmis nominatis.
XVI. IMAGO EST DELPHINI. utilis

---

70 Missing in the Vatican manuscript, but included in the corresponding passage from Plut. 44.35, 212v.

name,⁷¹ which is of the second magnitude.
Also, the Moon shall be trine or sextile the Sun. Jupiter and Mars shall both rise before the Sun at dawn,
or the Moon shall translate light between them by a trine or sextile. The malefics and Cauda Draconis shall be cadent.
It is engraved in emerald or diamond, most properly *alectoria*, or cast from gold.

THE FIFTEENTH IS AN IMAGE OF A FALLING VULTURE.⁷²
This has the power to confer eloquence when carried, and an agreeable audience. And it is imprinted when
the Sun, in its hour, rises under the stars of this image.
And Venus and Mercury shall be united with it, the Moon and Jupiter
trine or sextile to them; or the Moon shall be in the house of the Sun,
both Venus and Mercury sextile to it, Jupiter likewise
making the same aspect to them, together with the Moon, if it is fortunate.
The malefics and Cauda Draconis shall be cadent. It is cast from gold or silver, or inscribed in one
of the aforementioned gemstones.

THE SIXTEENTH IMAGE IS THAT OF A DOLPHIN,⁷³ useful for

---

71 That is, Altair, from *al-Ṭā'er*.
72 It is not entirely certain to which constellation this entry may correspond. The description of the image seems to be an erroneous recapitulation of Lyra, but the only northern Ptolemaic constellation for which Anselmi fails to include an identifiable entry is Cygnus (he conflates Pegasus and Equuleus into one), so Cygnus seems most likely here.
73 The constellation Delphinus.

piscatoribus, et nautis. dat enim illis gratiam capiendi
pisces, aggregans eos. nautas adiuvat cont-
ra maris, et fluminum pericula. Figuratur quidem
quotiens Sol sub eius imaginis stellas decurrens
horoscopat. cum illis Iupiter, et ☾ foelices, ambo
sint illi trigonae, vel exagonae, vel saltem transferat,
vel Solem a Iove, aut Mercurius Lunae trigone
vel exagone. sint quoque Venus, et Mercurius, foelices.
penitus vitentur malignae cum ☋. funditur ex
auro vel argento, aut imprimatur in aliqua
ex eis gemmis, quas diximus contra casus
nocivos, esse potentes, et contra pericula.
XVII. IMAGO EST EQUUS. SUNT AUTEM
DUO, PRIMUS, ET SECUNDUS. est vero posse istius
imaginis, ut eam deferens fortunam habeant,
et gratiam in bestiis domesticis, equitabilibus, et sub-
iugalibus, sive custodiam habeant, sive equitet. et praeservat haec ab infirmitatibus, et instanti curat.
Imprimitur cum Sol sub stellis eius decurrens

fishers and sailors; indeed, it grants them good fortune in catching
fish, gathering them together. It aids sailors against
the perils of the sea and rivers. The figure is made
when the Sun rises under the stars of this image,
when Jupiter and the Moon are favorable to them, both
trine or sextile the Sun, or at least so by translation of light,
either to the Sun from Jupiter, or Mercury to the Moon by a trine
or sextile. Mercury and Venus shall be fortunate as well.
The malefics and Cauda Draconis shall be avoided entirely. It is cast
    from
gold or silver, or engraved in one
of the gemstones which I have said are strong against accidental
injuries and hazards.

THE SEVENTEENTH IMAGE IS A HORSE, AND THERE
ARE TWO, THE FIRST AND THE SECOND.[74] And the power of this
image is such that one carrying it shall have good fortune
and influence with domestic beasts, those fit for riding and
putting under the yoke, whether caring for them or riding them, and
it preserves them from infirmities, and cures them expeditiously.
It is imprinted when the Sun, in its hour, rises under the stars of this
    image,

---

74 The constellations Equuleus and Pegasus.

horoscopat hora sua. et sint illi Mars, et ☽
illi exagoni, vel trigoni, sic et Iupiter. Saturnus
et Cauda cadant.
XVIII. Imago est Andromedae. et nominatur mulier catherata, quae non novit virum.
huius imago potens est instaurare, et reconciliare,
et dare amores mulierum. Imprimitur hora ☉
horoscopante eo cum stella quae primam sortita
est magnitudinem, et pingitur supra eius pedem.
et sit Venus foelix, et ☽ pariter, et trigone, vel
exagone, aut Luna sit Sol. malignae cadant.
Ultima est imago trianguli. huius est
posse conferre ad artium ingenia, et exercitia
et dare famam in geometria, aut arithmetica,
et mathematicis. Imprimitur decurrente sub ea
Sole, et horoscopante cum stellis eius hora sua,
vel fuerit ei Mercurius, aut Luna, quacumque harum
fuerit, sit illi Iupiter foelix, trigonus, vel exagonus,
vel quam horoscopare diximus summum teneat

GIORGIO ANSELMI / Brian Johnson

[23v]

and Mars and the Moon are
sextile or trine to it; Jupiter shall be likewise. Saturn
and Cauda Draconis shall be cadent.
THE EIGHTEENTH IMAGE IS ANDROMEDA, and it is called
"the woman enthroned, who has not known a man".
This image has the power to restore, and recover,
and grant the love of women. It is imprinted in the hour of the Sun,
when it rises with the first-magnitude star (of this image,
which is) depicted above her foot.
And Venus shall be fortunate, and the Moon likewise, and trine
or sextile (the Sun), or the Moon shall be placed with the Sun.[75] The
    malefics shall be cadent.
LAST IS THE IMAGE OF A TRIANGLE,[76] which has
the power to confer talent and skill in the arts,
and to grant fame in geometry or arithmetic,
and mathematics. It is imprinted
when the Sun, in its hour, rises under the stars of this image,
or Mercury or the Moon does.
Whichever, Jupiter shall be favorable to it, trine or sextile,
or such that, (the stars) rising as we have said, Jupiter occupies the
    midheaven,

---

75 Reading, with Plut. 44.35, 213v, *fit soli* for *sit sol*.
76 The constellation Triangulum.

Divinum Opus de Magia Disciplina

coelum, aut locum .xi. imprimitur autem in conve-
nienti gemma, vel funditur ex auro, vel argento.

Notificatio modorum imaginum quae fiunt sub stellis figurarum
quae a zodiaco tenent australem partem. capitulum .3.

Imagines orbis octavi quae sunt australis
sunt numera .15. Quarum prima est Caete, et est ma-
rinus piscis, super eius ventrem pingitur pisciculus
conversus. quidam super dorsu eius pingunt rudus
vel rubum grandem. et scripserunt quidam imaginem,
hanc habere serpentinus caput breve superius, et infe-
rius. huius est posse cum fusa fuerit ex auro
vel argento, aut impressa gemmae quae naturam sectatur stellarum benignarum, conferre foelici-
tatem, et fortunam grandem tam terra, quam mari.
maris item pericula, et fluminis prohibet, et tempestates
arcet. hominem prudentem facit, et amicabilem,
et amissa recuperat. Est autem compositionis tempus,
cum Sol horoscopat hora sua, cum eius stellis decurrens, praecipue cum ea quae secundam sortita est

GIORGIO ANSELMI / Brian Johnson

[24r]

or the eleventh house. And it is imprinted in an appropriate
gemstone, or cast from gold or silver.

> CHAPTER THREE: *A Note on the Methods Pertaining to
> Those Images Made Under the Stars of Those Figures
> Which Occupy the Region South of the Zodiac.*

The southerly images in the eighth sphere
are fifteen in number, THE FIRST OF WHICH IS CETUS, a
fish of the sea. Upon its belly is depicted a little inverted fish;
some depict upon its back a lump
or a great spine, and some have written that this image
has a little serpent head above and below.
This image has the power, when cast from gold
or silver, or engraved in a gemstone that naturally follows
the benign stars, to confer happiness,
and great fortune, on land as well as sea.
It likewise defends against the perils of ocean and river, and
keeps storms away. It makes a person prudent and amicable,
and restores what is lost. And the time of its composition is
when the Sun, in its hour, rises with the stars of this image,
especially with that which is of the second

magnitudinem, haec in eius ventre pingitur. Iupiter
autem Solem mane precedat in exortu. ☽ cum Iove,
Soli trigona, vel exagona. malignae cadant, et ☋.
2.ᵃ EST ORIONIS IMAGO. huius est
grande posse in litibus, et adversitatibus super-
antem facere, et in bellis victorem. haec ducibus
auxilium praestat, et militias dat famosam. figurat
autem cum decurrens Sol sub eius stellis horoscopat,
hora sua, proprie quidem cum altera duarum quae primam
sunt sortitae magnitudinem, altera quidem super
eius sinistrum pingitur humerum: super dextrum pedem
altera. ☿ sit noviter antecedens Solem in exortu,
♄ cum eo, aut illi trigonus, vel exagonus, cum recaeptione,
si fieri possunt. et utrique sit Sol Luna foelix, saltem
inter eos, et Solem trigone, vel exagone transferat.
siquidem sit opus cum ea quae super sinistrum pingitur humerum, Saturnus loco disponatur, Mars
cum Iove. funditur ex auro, vel argento, aut
impressio fit in aliqua ex gemmis nominatis

magnitude, depicted in the belly of the image,
and Jupiter shall rise before the Sun at dawn. The Moon shall be together with Jupiter,
trine or sextile the Sun. The malefics and Cauda Draconis shall be cadent.

SECOND IS THE IMAGE OF ORION. This has
great power in litigations, and surmounting adversities,
and making one victorious in wars; it
provides aid to commanders, and makes armies renowned. And it is fashioned
when the Sun, in its hour, rises under the stars of this image,
especially together with one of the two that
are of the first magnitude, namely that one depicted above
Orion's left shoulder—the other being above his right foot—
Mercury newly preceding the Sun at dawn.
Saturn shall be together with Mercury, or trine or sextile to it, with reception
if possible. And the Sun (and) Moon shall be favorable to each of them, at least
(by means of) the translation of light between them and the Sun by trine or sextile.
Since the work shall be done with the (star) depicted above the left
shoulder, Saturn shall be placed there. Mars
shall be together with Jupiter. It is cast from gold or silver, or
engraved in one of the gemstones named

ad haec, proprie vero in adamante, alectorio, vel chalcedonio.
3.ᵃ EST FLUMINIS IMAGO. haec potens
est subsidium ferre nautis, et piscatoribus. maris
et fluminum pericula prohibere. honores tribuit
et gestantis eam corpus sanum reddit, et praeservat,
praecipue autem a cholerae passionibus, et fortis
auxilii est curae. Compositio autem eius fit cum Sol
sub eius decurrens stellis horoscopat hora sua,
proprie quidem cum ea quae in eius pingitur littore primam
sortita magnitudinem. Iove ille trigono, vel exagono.
foelici sit et Luna. vitetur omnino malignarum
praesentia, et ♃. Imprimitur autem decenter in topatio
vel turcaide, et similibus virtute, aut funditur
ex auro, vel argento.
4.ᵃ EST LEPORIS IMAGO. huius est
posse facere ferentes se in parvorum animalium
custodia. posita vero sylvestris eas adgregat
bestiolas, praecipue lepores, cuniculos, et similes

for this purpose, but especially in diamond, *alectoria*,
or chalcedony.
THIRD IS THE IMAGE OF A RIVER.[77] This is a powerful
aid to be carried by sailors and fishers,
preventing the hazards of sea and river. It bestows honors,
and restores and preserves bodily health when carried,
but especially from choleric sufferings, and it is a powerful
help in case of trouble. And its composition shall be when the Sun,
in its hour, rises under the stars of this image,
especially with that one of the first magnitude which is depicted on
    its shore.
Jupiter shall be trine or sextile to it,
and the Moon fortunate. The presence of the malefics
and Cauda Draconis shall be avoided entirely. And it is properly
    engraved in topaz
or turquoise, and stones of similar virtue, or cast
from gold or silver.
FOURTH IS THE IMAGE OF A HARE.[78] This has
the power to make one a keeper of little animals when carried;
indeed, placed in the forest, it gathers together those
little beasts, especially hares, rabbits, and the like,

---

77 The constellation Eridanus.
78 The constellation Lepus.

et eas multiplicat. est rursus facere gestante
vitare facere, versutias, et fallacias, et dolos.
scribis famem dat, et honorem, et gratiam. componitur
autem cum Sole sub ea decurrit, et horoscopat hora
sua, et ☿ sit retrorsus incedans, aut cum Solis
radiis excandens, sed trigonus aut exagonus Iovi, et
item Lunae foelicibus, et si possible sit Venus.
malignae prorsus cadant, et ☋. Imprimitur autem in
adamante, berillo, vel zaphiro, aut funditur
ex auro, vel argento.
5.ª EST CANIS PRIORIS IMAGO. haec potens
est gestanti grandes honores conferre, et dignitates, et potentias. et si in eius compositione fuerit
mars foelix, ac fortis, fortem victorem in cunctis
facere. fortunam facit in gubernatione dome-
sticorum animalium, sed praecipue Canum. illos equidem
in sanitate conservat, et factis in eis morbis
auxilio curae fit, praecipue cum eis data in potu
fuerit aqua loturae sigilli, aut res sigillata cum eo.

and multiplies them. On the other hand, it is carried
to evade subterfuges, deceptions, and frauds.
It gives fame,[79] honor, and grace to scribes. And it is composed
when the Sun, in its hour, rises under this image.
And Mercury shall be moving retrograde, or
burned by the rays of the Sun, but trine or sextile Jupiter, and
likewise they shall both be favorable to the Moon, and if possible
    Venus shall be (as well).
The malefics shall be entirely cadent, along with Cauda Draconis.
    And it is engraved in
diamond, or beryl, or sapphire, or cast
from gold or silver.

FIFTH IS THE IMAGE OF THE GREAT DOG.[80] This has the power
to confer great honors, and dignities,
and powers when carried, and if Mars should be fortunate and
    strong in its composition,
it makes one a powerful victor in all matters.
It makes for good fortune in the management of domestic
animals, but especially of dogs; indeed,
it keeps them healthy, and aids in curing them of diseases,
especially when they are given water to drink
with which the image has been bathed, or some thing sealed with
    the image.

---

79 Reading, with Plut. 44.35, 215r, *famam* for *famem*.
80 The constellation Canis Major.

eos quoque mites, et placidos efficit eius praesentia
quantumlibet immanes sint, et feroces. fit vero
compositio eius, quotiens Sol decurrit cum stellis
imaginis, proprie sub ea horoscopante, quae primam sortita est magnitudinem, in eius picta est ore. est
vero illa sub qua decurrens Sol, dies efficit ca-
niculares, et nominatur Alabor, et Aschere, et Canis.
Sit quoque Iupiter Soli trigonus, vel exagonus, foelix. aut saltem
sit cum Venere, et Luna, et pari conspectu Luna
transferat inter eum, et Solem. Imprimitur autem,
aut funditur qualiter ante dicta.
6.ª EST CANIS MINOR, sive posterior.
haec potens est qualiter praemissa, sed infra, sic et
eius compositionis modus, et impressionis.
7.ª EST IMAGO HYDRAE. Dixerunt
figuram eius esse hydram, super cuius dorsus anterius
est vas, et super caudam corvus. huius est proprietas
gestantes astutum reddere, et futurorum providentes,
bonis omnibus abundantes. noxiis insistit caloribus.

Its presence likewise makes them mild and calm,
no matter how savage and ferocious they may be. But is shall be
composed when the Sun travels along with the stars
of this image, especially under the rising of that one which is of the first
magnitude, depicted in the dog's mouth;
indeed, it is the Sun's travel under that star which causes the dog days,
and it is called al-Abor, and Aschere, and "the dog".[81]
Also, Jupiter shall be trine or sextile the Sun, fortunate, or at least
together with Venus and the Moon, and the Moon
translating light between it and the Sun by the same aspect. And it is engraved
or cast as said previously.

SIXTH IS THE LITTLE DOG, or the "following (dog)".
This has the same power as the preceding, but less so, and so too
the manner of its composition and imprinting.

SEVENTH IS THE IMAGE OF HYDRA. They say
its form is that of a water snake, upon the foreback of which
is a vessel, and upon its tail a crow. This has the property
of granting one cunning when carried, and foresight of the future,
(and) abundance in all good things. It suppresses injurious heat,

---

[81] Most commonly known today as Sirius (actually Sirius A and B, the latter only distinguished in the nineteenth century).

propterea quod eius stellae sub ♋ noni orbis decurrunt.
nunc vero res alter se habet, etenim in praesentia
sub ♌ reponitur. Sola autem hydrae imago
potens est aggregare, et multiplicare, et movere
serpentes et reptilia, et eorum venena, et morsus,
et occursus prohibere, et curare. Imprimitur cum
Sol sub eius stellis decurrit, et horoscopat hora
sua. cum illis Iupiter, et Luna foelices, ambo illis
sint trigoni, vel exagoni. malignae cum ☋ cadant
et est proprie eius sculptura in lapide dragos
aut bezoar, vel auro, vel argento.
8.ª EST IMAGO CORVI, ET EST ADGREGANS
volatilia, ea multiplicans. eorum tamen nocumenta
prohibens, et damna. a linguis propterea detrahentium
et invidentium praeservat. et vero eius compositio
cum Sol ut in superiori horoscopat hora sua sub
stellis eius, praeciupue sub ea quae super eius sinistram
alam. imprimitur gemmae appropriatae, vel funditur
ex auro vel argento.

because its stars formerly traveled under Cancer in the ninth sphere;
now, however, it presides over another matter, since at present
it lies under Leo. By itself, the image of Hydra
has the power to gather, and multiply, and move
serpents and reptiles, and avert their venoms, and bites,
and attacks, and to cure these. It is imprinted when
the Sun, in its hour, rises under the stars of this image,
when both Jupiter and the Moon are favorable to them, both of these
trine or sextile to them. The malefics and Cauda Draconis shall be cadent.
And it is properly sculpted in *dragos* stone
or bezoar, or gold or silver.
EIGHTH IS THE IMAGE OF A CROW,[82] and it makes flying creatures flock together,
and multiply, but prevents them from being a nuisance
and causing damage: therefore is protects against disparaging
and envious tongues. And indeed it is composed
when the Sun, as previously, rises in its hour under
the stars of this image, especially under that which is above the crow's left
wing. It is engraved in an appropriate gemstone, or cast
from gold or silver.

---

82 The constellation Corvus.

9.ª EST IMAGO NAVIS. haec imago nautis
perutilis est, conservans eorum illaesa navigia, et
velocia efficiens cursu, et a periculis maris praeservans. item, et fluminum pericula prohibet. insuper
gestanti magnos praestat honores, famam, gratiam
divitias, et bona. Compositio eius cum Sol sub ea
decurrit, hora sua horoscopans, proprie cum stella
primam sortita magnitudinem, quae super eius remi
quis pingitur, et nominata est Suchel, et Canopus.
Sit vero Iupiter mane antecedens Solem in exortu,
et alter foelix, et Soli trigonus, vel exagonus, aut Venus
sit et luna. vel transferat inter hos trigone,
vel exagone. malignae cadant, Saturnus praecipue,
et Cauda, nisi fortasse foelix existat. et sit
Iovi foelici trigonus, vel exagonus. Sit vero eius impressio in quadam ex gemmis quarum proprietas est conser-
vare a nocitivis casibus, aut funditur ex
auro vel argento.
X.ª EST IMAGO CENTAURI, QUAE POTENS

NINTH IS THE IMAGE OF A SHIP.[83] This image is very useful for sailors, preserving their ships from harm, and making for a swift voyage, and protecting them from the perils of the sea, and likewise warding off riverine hazards. In addition, it bestows great honors, fame, grace, riches, and good things when carried. It is composed when the Sun, in its hour, rises under this image, especially along with the first-magnitude star which is depicted above the Ship's oar, and is called Suchel,[84] and Canopus. But Jupiter and the other benefic shall rise before the Sun at dawn, and be trine or sextile the Sun, or Venus and the Moon shall do so, or (the Moon) shall translate light between them by trine or sextile. The malefics shall be cadent, especially Saturn, and Cauda Draconis, unless perhaps (one) should be fortunate, and trine or sextile a fortunate Jupiter. But it is engraved in one of the gemstones having the virtue of protecting against accidental injuries, or cast from gold or silver.

TENTH IS THE IMAGE OF A CENTAUR,[85] which has the power

---

83 The constellation Argo Navis.
84 Arabic *Suhel/Suhayl*.
85 The constellation Centaurus.

est gestantes gratum inter homines reddere bene, et
honeste perseverantes, virginitatem praeservat.
venatori ad praedam ultimo fit adiutorio. Est vero
compositionis temporis, hora Solis, vel sub ea decurrens,
cum eius stellis horoscopat. Sit autem Iupiter mane
illum antecedens in exortu, aut illi adiunctus
trigone, vel exagone. et itidem Luna, vel transferens
inter eos horum alterius conspectu. et sit Venus
Iovi pariter commixta. cum Sole Mercurius.
malignis, et ☋, cadentibus. Est vero imaginis huius
figura centauri, in cuius sinistra est cultellus, cui
lepus suspenditur. Sub dextro tenet bachulum collo,
ex quo suspensa pedibus bestiola pendet.
XI. EST LUPI IMAGO. haec prohibet
vorantium ferarum, et rabidarum incursus, et occursus,
praecipue quidem luporum, eos domesticabiles eius
efficit praesentia. et adgregat detrahenti vim.
linguas quietat. cum malignarum altera in eius
compositione horoscopat, aut sit illi diametra,

GIORGIO ANSELMI/Brian Johnson

[27v]

to restore goodwill among people when carried, and
make honor endure, and preserve virginity.
It is made as a final aid to the hunter in taking their prey. But
the time of its composition is the hour of the Sun, or when it
rises under the stars of this image. And Jupiter shall
rise before the Sun at dawn, or aspect it
by a trine or sextile, and the Moon shall do likewise, or translate light
between them by another aspect, and Venus shall
be together with Jupiter as well. Mercury shall be together with the Sun.
The malefics and Cauda Draconis shall be cadent. But the form of this image
is that of a centaur, in whose left hand is a knife, from which
a hare is suspended. He holds the neck of a staff with his right hand,
from which a little beast hangs by its feet.
ELEVENTH IS THE IMAGE OF A WOLF.[86] This wards off
the attacks of voracious and rabid beasts, and prevents one from meeting with them,
especially wolves. Its presence makes them domesticable,
and gathers them together, taking away their strength,
quieting their tongues. When one of the malefics is rising in its
composition, (however,) or opposing or squaring the ascendant,

---

86 The constellation Lupus.

vel tetragona, furentes facit, et rabidos. et
animantia, quoque occurunt lacerantes, et ha-
bitationum loca perturbantes. et nisis fiat qualiter
dicemus ad fugandas. compositionis autem tempus
est Solis hora, quotiens cum stellis eius horoscopat,
aut Luna. et sunt ambo ipsa luminaria per
mixta trigone vel exagone. Sic et Iupiter, aut saltem eorum
altero conspectu transferat luna inter eos.
malignae prorsus cadant, et ♋. funditur ex auro,
vel argento, vel in aliqua ex dictis gemmis.
XII. EST LARIS IMAGO. haec malorum
demonum prohibet incursus. Se gestantes confortat,
vigorem praebet, et potentem in eorum advocationem
reddit, facit etiam ut accedant, et obediant.
Compositio eius est cum Sol horoscopat hora sua cum
illis stellis, Iupiter autem illi permixtus trigone,
vel exagone, Luna pariter, aut sit loco Solis.
Venus etiam illi trigona, vel exagona. Imprimatur
in onichino, vel gihazaha.

it makes them rabid and raging, and
even incites them to rush in, rending and
wrecking places of habitation. And unless it should be made as
we have just said, it is for chasing them away: the time of its composition
is the hour of the Sun, when it rises along with the stars of this image,
or the Moon does so, and both of those luminaries form
a mixed trine or sextile. Jupiter shall do likewise, or
the Moon shall at least translate light between (it and the Sun) by another aspect.
The malefics shall be entirely cadent, as well as Cauda Draconis. It is cast from gold
or silver, or engraved in one of the aforementioned gemstones.
TWELFTH IS THE IMAGE OF A SEABIRD.[87] This prevents
the attacks of wicked demons. When carried, it strengthens one,
provides vigor, and makes one's counsel seem strong,
such that (others) even assent and obey.
It is composed when the Sun, in its hour, rises with
the stars of this image, and Jupiter makes a mixed trine or sextile to it,
the Moon doing likewise, or (the Moon) shall be in the house of the Sun.
Venus shall also be trine or sextile (the Sun).[88] It is engraved
in onyx or *gihazaha*.[89]

---

87 *laris* here is probably a scribal mistake for *aris*, in which case this is actually the constellation Ara, the altar.
88 Ambiguous syntax makes the object in question here uncertain.
89 Compare *gihagaha* at 19r, above.

XIII. ET ULTIMA EST AUSTRALIS CORONAE
imago. haec gestanti potens est honores, et dignitates conferre, famam, fortunam, gratiam
cum regibus, et faciles impetrationes ab eis. Compositio quidem fit hora Solis. et eo cum stellis
eius horoscopante. Iove quidem illi trigono
vel exagono pariter, et Luna. et sit Iupiter dominator
coeli summi, aut locum eum foelix tenens. et semper
sint ambo luminaria trigona vel exagona,
et foelicia, et fortia. vitentur vero malignae cum ☋.
Imprimitur autem in gemma ex appropriatis, aut funditur ex auro vel argento. Non minus tamen
sunt modi compositionis hanc ad nocecndum, et non
dicimus eos singulariter, cum exempla plurima
posita sunt. etenim in eis semper malignae potentes
fiunt, et foelices in quarum est omnis motus. contra
benignae cadentes, et in foelices quibus nullus est
motus.

[28v]

THIRTEENTH AND LAST IS THE IMAGE OF THE SOUTHERN CROWN.[90]

This has the power to confer honors and dignities when carried, fame, fortune, the goodwill of kings, and swift fulfillment of petitions to them. In any case, its composition is in the hour of the Sun, when it rises with the stars of this image, at least when Jupiter and the Moon are trine or sextile to it as well. And Jupiter shall be lord of the midheaven, or occupying a fortunate place. And both luminaries shall always be trine or sextile, and fortunate and strong, but the malefics and Cauda Draconis shall be avoided. And it is engraved in an appropriate gemstone, or cast from gold or silver. No fewer, however, are the methods of composing this image to cause injury, and we are not speaking of them in detail, with many examples given, because in such images the malefics are always made strong, and favorable to those things in which all (the image's) motive force lies; conversely, the benefics shall be cadent, and favorable to those things in which (the image) has no motive force.

---

90 The constellation Corona Australis.

Divinum Opus de Magia Disciplina

[29r]

De modis componendi imagines quae non sunt stellate, sed concomitantes signorum xii. Capitulum .4.

Ultra modos imaginum quarum diximus
modos, sunt imagines quas greci philosophi, et indi, et
arabes dixerunt concomitari praedictas, et enim
habent haec figurationes suas ex stellis qualiter
illae. earum vero modos in universalibus
diximus, et figurationes. hoc loco restat
nobis proprietates earum quarundam, et compositionis modos describe. et quoque vis in hac
compositione dicatur qui fiat impressio quotiens ☽
decurrit cum stellis huius, aut illius imaginis.
Si tamen eadem est ratione de Sole dicendum,
et item de stella alia foelici, aut infoelici,
benigna, aut maligna, secundum exigentiam
motus accidentis, quae imago motiva est,
ex artificis intentione.
IMAGINIS COMPOSITIONE cuius est posse curare
choleram, et ventris dolores, et ab hiis gestantes

GIORGIO ANSELMI/Brian Johnson

[29r]

CHAPTER FOUR: *On the Methods of Composing Images Which Are Not Stellar, But Accompany the Twelve Signs.*

Beyond the methods pertaining to the images of which we have spoken,
there are images which the Greek, and Indian, and
Arab philosophers have said accompany the aforementioned, and indeed
these have their own figurations according to the stars, just as
those (others do). While we have spoken in general of their methods and figurations, in this part it remains
for us to describe the properties and methods of composition of some of them,
and the power of each in this
composition, the imprint of which is said to be made when the Moon
travels with the stars thereof, or its image.
If, however, the same reckoning should to be applied to the Sun,
and likewise to some other star, favorable or unfavorable,
benign or malign, according to the demands
of the accident to be moved, of which the image is the mover,
that is up to the intention of the artificer.
THE COMPOSITION OF AN IMAGE that has the power to cure
cholera, and pains of the stomach, and to preserve one from these when carried.

Divinum Opus de Magia Disciplina

praeservare. Est imago homini sedens in harena
et promentis manus suas, super ventrem suum. fit
autem cum ☽ decurrit sub stellis quae figurantur
sub cauda minoris ursae, et super pectus
mulieris quae non novit virum. et sint illi
trigoni Iupiter, et Venus, aut exagoni. malignae cadant
et ☋. contra vero provocat nimios hos
dolores cum sub ea Saturnus decurrit, et fuerit
Mars illi, aut Mercurius diameter, vel
tetragonus. et si fuerit horum alter, aut Saturnus
dominator supra radicem octavae domus
erit deterius.

IMAGINIS COMPOSITIONE prohibens latronem
ab ingressu domus. est figura hominis in harena sedentis,
et clamantis ad latrones. fit autem cum stellae
horoscopant imaginis cuius exortu concomitatur,
et cum hiis ☽ foelix trigona vel exagona Soli proprie,
et benignis. cadant cum ☋ malignae. Siquidem
contrario fiunt ut horoscopet Mercurius, et

GIORGIO ANSELMI / Brian Johnson

[29v]

It is the image of a man sitting in the sand
and holding his hands over his belly. And it is made
when the Moon travels under the stars arranged
beneath the tail of the Little Bear, and above the breast
of the woman who has not known a man,[91] and
Jupiter and Venus shall be trine or sextile to it. The malefics and
    Cauda Draconis shall be cadent.
But conversely, these stars provoke an excess of those
pains when Saturn travels under them, and
Mars or Mercury oppose or
square them. And if one of these or Saturn
should be lord over the root of the eighth house,[92]
it will be even worse.
THE COMPOSITION OF AN IMAGE to prevent a bandit
from entering a house. It is the figure of a man sitting in the sand
and yelling at some bandits, and it is made when the stars
of this image rise with the dawn,
especially with a fortunate Moon trine or sextile the Sun
and the benefics. The malefics and Cauda Draconis shall be
    cadent. If,
conversely, it is made so that Mercury and Mars are rising,

---

91 Presumably Virgo.
92 I.e., one of these planets rules the sign in the eighth house of the elected chart.

Divinum Opus de Magia Disciplina

Mars, aut diametri sint, aut tetragoni.
horoscopantae Lunae. et cadens Iupiter. semper
erit domus latronibus perturbatu, et confusa
et damnata.
UT AUTEM NON INCENDATUR IGNIS IN DOMO.
fiat imago hora ☽. et ea cum dictis stellis
horoscopante, praesentibus benignis trigonis,
vel exagonis. et absentibus malignis cum ☋. Est
autem clamatis hominis propter ignem figura. quae si contra
fuerit, loco Lunae sit Mars, aut diameter, vel
tetragonus illi et cadant benignae. facit domum
in qua fuerit ignis conburens.
ALTERIUS IMAGINIS AD IDEM, HIC EST MODUS.
Imprimatur figura hominis cuius faciei figura similis
sit figurae canis, cuius sinistra manus tenet suc-
censum candelabrum, secundum modum praedictae. Sed
dicat {dicat}[93] artifex, Quacumque in domo fuerit haec
imago incendatur ignis. vel quae sit extinctum candelabrum,
et non poterit in ea ignis accendi. sepeliatur in medio domus.

---

93 Duplication error in the manuscript.

GIORGIO ANSELMI/*Brian Johnson*

[30r]

or opposing or squaring
the rising Moon, and Jupiter is cadent,
the house shall be constantly disturbed, and confounded,
and surrendered to bandits.
BUT SO THAT FIRE SHOULD NOT IGNITE IN A HOUSE,
an image shall be made in the hour of the Moon, as it rises with the aforementioned stars,
trine or sextile the presence of the benefics,
and the malefics and Cauda Draconis shall be absent (from any aspect with them). And it is
the figure of a man crying out next to a fire, which—if, on the contrary,
Mars is in the house of the Moon, or opposing or
squaring it, and the benefics cadent—shall make the house
in which it is put be consumed by fire.
HERE IS THE METHOD OF ANOTHER IMAGE FOR THE SAME:
Imprint the figure of a man, the form of whose face is like
that of a dog, whose left hand grasps a burning
candelabrum, after the manner aforesaid. But
the artificer shall say, *(should) this image be anywhere in a house*
that a flame may be kindled, or where there may be an extinguished candelabrum,
it shall not be possible for fire to be kindled there. The image shall be buried in the middle of the house.

Divinum Opus de Magia Disciplina

IMAGO cuius praesentia non impediunt
serpentes, neque reptilia loca, sed fugiunt, et
moriuntur. Fit serpentis imago quotiens Luna
horoscopat cum stellis capitis Algol. Dicat artifex,
Non remaneant serpentes, neque reptilia ubi
fuerit haec imago, diffugiant, moriantur. Et
sepeliatur in angulis .4.^{r} loci. Contrario
vero cum sub illis stellis decurrit Saturnus,
aut Lunam damnat diameter, aut tetragonus,
et hora sua, et cum eo ☋. Dicat artifex,
Congregentur serpentes, et multiplicentur in hoc
loco, aut super hanc imaginem, et accurrent.
Eiusdem, et paris est potentie IMAGO
facta cum ☽ fuerit horoscopans, cum stellis aquarii
initio perveniet ad exortum. Dicat artifex,
Recedat serpentes omnis, et omne reptile. et sepeliatur ut supra.
ALTERA EST AD IDEM IMAGO. cum horoscopat
Luna cum stellis quae cum cauda leporis pervenit

GIORGIO ANSELMI / Brian Johnson

[30v]

AN IMAGE, by the presence of which neither serpents nor reptiles shall obstruct a place, but flee and die. The image of a serpent is made when the Moon rises with the stars of Caput Algol. The artificer shall say, *neither serpents nor reptiles shall remain where this image is, they shall scatter and die.* And it is to be buried in the four corners of the place. On the contrary, however, when Saturn, in its hour, travels under those stars, or condemns the Moon by opposition or square, and is together with Cauda Draconis, the artificer shall say, *serpents shall rush to congregate and multiply in this place, or upon this image.*
Likewise, and of equal power, is an IMAGE made when the Moon rises with the first star of Aquarius. The artificer shall say, *all serpents and every reptile shall retreat.* And it is to be buried as aforesaid.
ANOTHER IMAGE FOR THE SAME: When the Moon rises with the stars of the Hare's tail[94]

---

94 This would roughly correspond to the star θ Lepus.

ad exortum, et postremo navis, siquidem loco
Lunae sint. Saturnus autem illi diameter aut
tetragonis. Imago erit potens adgregandum,
et multiplicandum illa.
IMAGO DIABOLI. haec est potens
demones perturbare, comovere, exagitare,
et infestare eum cuius nomine facta fuerit, aut
domum in qua posita sit, et loca. Est autem
ut fiat figura diaboli vexantis hominem, aut locum.
Fit autem cum Sol horoscopat hora Saturni cum stellis
capitis Algol. et fuerit illi Saturnus infoelix
adiunctus, aut tetragonus, et ☋. benignae cadant.
Dicat artifex, Perturbet diabolus hunc hominem
et nominet, neque sinat illum vel paululum quiescere,
aut domum, vel locum. et si voluerit demonem
dicat. Accedat huc demon, respondeat,
obediat. et tunc in eius compositione fit sola figura
diaboli. ponatur sub lecto, vel loco, aut
limine domus, vel servetur ad tempus. Contra

GIORGIO ANSELMI / *Brian Johnson*

[31r]

and the Ship's stern[95] in
its house, and Saturn opposing or
squaring it, the image will have the power to gather together
and multiply those (creatures).
THE IMAGE OF A DEVIL: This has the power
to make demons disturb, agitate, harass,
and vex the one in whose name it is made, or
the house or location in which it is placed. And this is
how the figure of a devil is made to trouble a person or place:
The Sun shall be rising in the hour of Saturn, along with the stars
of Caput Algol, and an infortunate Saturn
conjoining or squaring it along with Cauda Draconis. The benefics
   shall be cadent.
The artificer shall say, *a demon shall disturb this person*, naming (the
   victim), *or this house, or place,*
not allowing them even a little rest.
And if one wishes, say to the demon,
come here, demon, respond,
obey. And therefore the image shall comprise only the figure
of a devil. It shall be placed under the bed, or (another) place, or
the threshold of the house, or kept in reserve for (some appropriate)
   time. On the contrary,

---

95 Comprising the modern constellation Puppis, a constituent of Argo Navis.

vero demones fugat, et ab eorum liberat incursu.
Cum fit imago fugientis diaboli, hora Solis,
decurrentis sub imaginis ea, et horoscopantis
et Iupiter fuerit illi tetragonus vel exagonus, foelix sit
et Luna utrique eorum altero conspectuum permixta.
sed malignae prorsus cadant, et ☋. Dicat artifex,
Diffugiat hinc omnis diabolus, non audeat hunc
hominem, domum, vel locum infestare, aut exagitare, vel perturbare.
IMAGINIS MODUS cuius est efficare congregare
et multiplicare, et fortunare capras, et oves,
et huiusmodi animantia. Fit ♈ imago, cum
fuerit ☽ sub ♈, proprieque sub eius .3.ª facie horoscopante. sintque Sol, ac Iupiter, et Venus foelices
eam ex trigono, vel exagono intuentes. fiat imago
Caprae, vel ovis. et dicat artifex in eius compositione,
et repositione stabuli, vel pascui, Multiplicentur
vel proficiatur caprae, vel reliqua in istis locis.
Contrario, ad nocendum illis. Sed loco Lunae

however, to make demons flee, and to be delivered from their attacks,
the image of a fleeing devil shall be made in the hour of the Sun,
when it rises under that image,[96]
and Jupiter is trine[97] or sextile to it, fortunate,
and the Moon makes another mixed aspect to both of them.
But the malefics shall be entirely cadent, as well as Cauda Draconis.
The artificer shall say,
every devil shall flee from this place, not daring
to vex, or harass, or disturb this person, house, or place.
THE METHOD FOR AN IMAGE which has the power to gather together,
and multiply, and make fortunate goats, and sheep,
and creatures of this sort: An image of Aries shall be made when
the Moon is under Aries, and especially rising under its third decan,
and the Sun, Jupiter, and Venus shall be favorable to
it by trine or sextile aspects. It shall be the image
of a goat or sheep, and the artificer shall say, during its composition
and placement in a stable or pasture, *goats shall be multiplied or benefited,*
or shall remain in those places.
On the contrary, to cause injury to them, Saturn shall be[98] in the house of the Moon,

---

96 Presumably Caput Algol again.
97 Reading, with Plut. 44.35, 219r, *trigonus* for *tetragonus*.
98 Reading, with Plut. 44.35, 219v, *sit* for *sed*.

Divinum Opus de Magia Disciplina

[32r]

Saturnus, aut intueatur eam ex diametro,
vel tetragono. Sit cum eo Mercurius. benignae cadant.
IMAGO cuius praesentia neque possunt
neque audent inimici ingredi civitatem, aut
locum vi, vel fraude. Fit autem cum fuerit ☽
decurrens sub stellis quae pinguntur in loco absci-
ssionis tauri, et ubi est cursus aquae fluminis,
et sint ♃, et ♂ illi adiuncti foelices trigoni
vel exagoni. est autem figura hominis tenentis sinistra
ensem evaginatum, et duos habens cereos super spatulas.
Dicat artifex, Non valeat, et audeat quisque
ex pugnare hanc civitatem, aut locum ingredi
vi, et sepeliatur in locis civitatis.
Consimilis posse, et virtutis IMAGO EQUITIS
in manu lanceam tenentis. est quoque haec potens ad
dandum gestanti victoram. est autem eius compositionem quotiens ☽
decurrit sub stellis quae pictae sunt super gladio Persei,
et capite Algol. Dicat artifex, Non audeat homo
insurgere, vel ex pugnare hunc locum, neque possit aut

GIORGIO ANSELMI / Brian Johnson

or aspecting it by opposition
or square. Mercury shall be together with Saturn. The benefics shall
    be cadent.
AN IMAGE by the presence of which enemies neither can
nor dare to enter a city or
place, either by force or deception: And it shall be made when the
    Moon
travels under the stars which appear in the place
where Taurus is interrupted by the course of the river of water,[99]
and Jupiter and Mars shall aspect it favorably by trine
or sextile. And it is the figure of a person holding in their left hand
an unsheathed sword, and having two wax tapers above their
    shoulders.
The artificer shall say, *no one shall be able, nor dare,*
to enter this city through battle, or this place
by force, and the image is to be buried in the locale of a city.
Of similar power and virtue, THE IMAGE OF A KNIGHT
holding a lance in their hand also has the power to
bestow victory when carried, and it is composed when the Moon
travels under the stars which appear above the sword of Perseus
and Caput Algol. The artificer shall say, *no person shall dare, nor be*
    able, to
enter this place, even through battle, or

---

99 I.e., where Taurus meets Eridanus.

hunc hominem superare, sed prosternatur, et repellatur cum op-
probrio, et damno. Contrario autem fient imagines ad nocendum loco, aut hominis. sint ambo ♂ et ♄ sub loco
Lunae aut illi diametri, vel tetragoni, Mars praecipue
et fortis. et dicat artifex, Succumbat hic populus,
aut homo, neque valeat, aut sciat, seu possit se tutari,
capiatur locus ab inimicis, et populetur, et destruatur.
IMAGO cuius est posse reddere gestantes
aptum ad omnes clavaturas aperiendum, quando clavaturae
supposita fuerit. Sit autem cum fuerit horoscopans ☾ decurrens sub stellis quae pinguntur sub sinistra manu
Cassiopeae. Est autem figura eius viri cuius est similis facies canis,
in dextro quam erigit tenet claves, et in altera candelam.
Dicat artifex, Aperiatur omnis clavatura quam haec
imago tetigerit. et sint in eius trigono vel exagono
benignae foelices.
IMAGO cuius praesentia non movetur canis adversus hominem, neque latrat. Figura est canis imago
cuius os sit revolutus ad caudam, quotiens ☾ horoscopat

to overcome this person, but shall be laid prostrate, and driven away, suffering
opprobrium and loss. On the contrary, however, should images be made to cause
injury to a place or person, both Mars and Saturn shall be in the house
of the Moon, or opposing or squaring it, especially Mars,
(which shall be) strong. And the artificer shall say, *this community or person shall surrender, having neither the strength, nor knowledge, nor ability to defend themselves,*
the place captured by enemies, and laid waste, and destroyed.
AN IMAGE which has the power when carried to render
all locks ready to be opened, whenever a lock
is subjected to it: And it shall be fashioned when the Moon rises
under the stars which appear beneath the left hand
of Cassiopeia. And its figure is that of a man whose face is like that of a dog,
holding keys in his raised right hand, and a candle in the other.
The artificer shall say, *every lock which this*
image touches shall open. And in its (composition)
the benefics shall favor (the Moon)[100] by trine or sextile.
AN IMAGE by the presence of which a dog will not come toward
nor bark at a person: The image of a dog
whose mouth is turned toward its tail is fashioned when the Moon rises

---

[100] The text is ambiguous as to what the benefics are aspecting, but the position of the Moon appears to be the determining factor for this image.

decurrens sub stellis minoris ursae. et dicat artifex,
Non moveatur, neque latret omnino canis. Eadem
est vis imaginis canis facta, cum fuerit ☽ decurrens
sub stellis quae posteriora, et ilia figuratur ♈,
et cum illis horoscopans. Dicat artifex, Latret
omnis canis ad huius praesentiam, siquidem facta fuerit
canis imago, sed os eius collario conclusus. et
hoc cum ☽ locum intuta diametro, vel tetragono,
sub signo muto decurrit. Dicat artifex,
Latret canis, sed mutus fiat.
Imago cuius praesentia, moratur equus non per-
transiens ubi sculpta fuerit. est imago equi, et
hoc cum ☽ decurrit sub stellis quae super dextrum
Persei pedem, et humerum retinentis habenas, hora
sua cum illis horoscopans. Dicat artifex, Equus
quicumque super hanc transierit, moratur faciet. Sepeliatur in loco transitus equorum.
Imago quae loco reposita facit ut
nullus animal in eo moratur faciat, sed inde diffugiat,

under the stars of the Little Bear. And the artificer shall say,
no dog shall move, nor bark at all. Of the same
power is the image of a dog fashioned when the Moon rises
under the stars which comprise the posterior and flanks of Aries.
The artificer shall say,
no[101] dog shall bark in the presence of this, when an image is fashioned
of a dog, but its mouth confined by a collar, and
this done when the Moon aspects[102] (the aforementioned)[103] place by opposition or square,
traveling under a mute sign.[104] The artificer shall say,
no[105] dog shall bark, but shall be silent.
AN IMAGE by the presence of which a horse is halted, (so as) not to
pass through where the image is sculpted: It is the image of a horse, and
this (is fashioned) when the Moon rises with the stars which are above
the right foot and shoulder of Perseus, (those) of the holder of the reins,[106]
in the Moon's hour. The artificer shall say,
any horse passing over this image shall be made to halt. It is to be buried
in a place through which horses travel.
AN IMAGE which, deposited in a place, makes it so that
no animal shall be made to halt there, but rather will flee that place

---

101 Interpolating, with Plut. 44.35, 220v, *non* before *latret*. The syntax of the entire passage seems somewhat awkward either way, but it becomes self-contradictory without this emendation.
102 Reading *intuita* for *intuta*.
103 The text is ambiguous as to what place the Moon is aspecting, but it would presumably be either the region of Aries or that of Ursa Minor adduced in the preceding instructions for the same end.
104 I.e., the water triplicity, Cancer, Pisces, and Scorpio.
105 Again interpolating *non*.
106 Presumably Auriga.

quasi flagello percussus. fit autem cum horoscopat Luna
hora sua cum stellis quae figurantur in pectori maioris
ursae, et ♌ dimidio. est vero figura imaginis hominis tenentis flagellum, et animalia percutientis. Dicat artifex,
Non morentur in hoc loco animalia, sed diffugiant
flagellata. sepeliatur in loco. fiat item flagellum
Luna disposita sicut praedicitur, et est potens. Dicat
artifex, Timeant animalia flagelli huius praesentiam
et fugiatur, non morentur.
IMAGO quae loco quovis disposita fa-
cit ut omnis asellus super transiens moretur, et
elata cervice rudiat. fiat imago cum decurrit ☽ sub stellis maioris ursae, quae pinguntur sub sinistra Cancri. et sepeliatur in loco
transitus, aut eorum mora. et dicat artifex,
Non transeat asellus super hanc imaginem, quin faciat
moratur, et alte rudiat.
IMAGO cuius est vis, ut quovis in loco posita
vel sepulta fuerit, boves omnes, et tauri super transeuntes,

as though struck by a whip: And it shall (be fashioned) when the Moon rises,
in its hour, with the stars that appear in the heart of the Great Bear, and aligns with the middle of Leo. But the form of the image is that of a person
holding a whip and striking animals. The artificer shall say, *animals shall not loiter in this place, but flee (as though) whipped.* The image is to be buried in the (desired) place. A whip
(made when) the Moon is disposed as aforesaid would be of similar (effect), and powerful:
The artificer shall say, *animals shall fear the presence of this whip, and flee without halting.*
AN IMAGE which, deposited in any place, makes it
so that every ass passing over it shall halt, and,
relieved of its burden, bray: The image shall be (fashioned) when the Moon travels under the stars of the Great Bear which appear above[107] the left side of Cancer, and it is to be buried in a place through which (asses) travel or loiter. And the artificer shall say, *an ass shall not pass over this image without being made to halt, and bray loudly.*
AN IMAGE which has the power, in whatever place it is deposited or buried, to cause all the cattle and bulls that pass over it

---

107 I.e., to the north of, reading *super* for *sub*.

stent et boent. fit imago ♉, cum ☽ sub stellis
decurrens, quae super draconis caudam pingitur, et
capite ♍, et horoscopat hora sua, et sepeliatur.
et dicat artifex, Congregentur tauri super hanc
imagine, et stent, et boent.
Imago quae facit ut ferae circum stantes
super eam congregetur, et stent. figuratur cum Luna
fuerit decurrens sub stellis minoris ursae, et an-
tecedentis Geminarum, et horoscopat hora sua.
Dicat artifex, Non remaneat fera in circuitu
sed veniant omnes, et congregentur super hanc imaginem.
est autem figura eius ursae.
Imago faciens aves congregari in loco repo-
sitionis eius, praecipue quidem corvos. figuretur imago
corvi quotiens ☽ decurrit sub stellis quae pinguntur in
pectore maioris ursae, et ♌ dimidio. et reponitur in loco volatus. et dicat artifex,
Congregentur corvi super hanc imaginem
et tumultum faciant.

to stop and bellow: It shall be an image of Taurus, (fashioned) when the Moon
rises with the stars which appear over the tail of the dragon[108] and
the head of Virgo, in the hour of the Moon, and the image shall be buried.
And the artificer shall say, *bulls shall congregate over this*
image, and stop and bellow.
AN IMAGE which makes beasts
congregate over it, standing around it: It shall be fashioned when the Moon
rises with the stars of the Little Bear,
preceding those of Gemini, in the hour of the Moon.
The artificer shall say, *no beast shall continue wandering,*
but all shall come and congregate over this image.
And its form is that of a bear.
AN IMAGE causing birds to congregate in the place
where it is kept, especially ravens: The image
of a raven is fashioned when the Moon travels under the stars which appear
in the heart of the Great Bear, and aligns with the middle of Leo. And
it shall be kept in a place where they might take flight. And the artificer shall say,
ravens shall congregate over this image
and make a commotion.

---

[108] In context, this can only be referring to Hydra.

IMAGO ut aves domesticae, et gallinae
congregentur ad aliquem locum, et cantent. figuratur
imago gallinae quotiens fuerit ☽ decurrens sub stellis
quae casus aquae ex urna ♒ pictae sunt, et hora
sua cum illis horoscopans, et loco ponatur. dicat
artifex, Congregentur gallinae vel aves super hanc imaginem.
IMAGO ad capiendum piscium multitudinem.
figuratur imago piscis, cum fuerit ☽ decurrens sub
stellis incurvati circa eius pedem, et humerum, et
brachium dextrum, hora sua cum stellis horoscopans.
alligetur rheti. Dicat artifex, Congregentur
pisces lacus huius, aut fluminis aut maris sub hac rhete.
IMAGO ut ex lacu aut flumine dif-
fugiant pisces. figuretur imago canis, et vorantis
et capientis pisces, quotiens fuerit ☽ decurrens sub stellis
quae pinguntur supra initium defluxus fluminis
ex urna ♒, cum illis horoscopans hora sua.
Dicat artifex, fugiant et moriantur pisces huius loci,
omnes ad imaginis huius praesentiam, et

GIORGIO ANSELMI / Brian Johnson

[34v]

AN IMAGE which makes domestic birds and hens
congregate in some place and sing:
The image of a hen shall be fashioned when the Moon rises with the stars
which depict the waters falling from the urn of Aquarius, and (this is done)
in the hour of the Moon, and it shall be deposited in the place (desired).
The artificer shall say, *hens and birds shall congregate over this image.*
AN IMAGE for catching a multitude of fish:
The image of a fish is fashioned when the Moon rises with
the stars curving around his[109] right foot, and shoulder, and
arm, in the hour of the Moon,
(and the fish shall be depicted) bound by a net. The artificer shall say,
the fish of this lake, or river, or sea shall congregate under this net.
AN IMAGE to make fish flee from a lake or river:
The image of a dog, devouring
and seizing fish, shall be fashioned when the Moon rises with the stars
which appear over the beginning of the river flowing
from the urn of Aquarius, in the hour of the Moon.
The artificer shall say, *all the fish of this place to which this image is presented shall flee and die*, and

---

109 Presumably referring to Aquarius again.

proiiciatur in flumine, aut lacu.
IMAGINIS modus quo ager prohibetur a cultura.
figuretur imago vomeris fracti, cum fuerit ☽
decurrens sub stellis quae super caput ♍ figuratur,
et cum illis horoscopat hora sua. Dicat artifex,
non intret vomer in hance glebam, et quae imissus
fuerit rumpatur. sepeliatur in .4. angulis agri.
IMAGO quae cum reposita fuerit in loco vendi-
tionis rerum, vel in apotheca, sive ad pondus, sive
ad mensura non vendatur. figuretur imago
viri in cuius sinistra manu est statera, aut sextarius,
dextra vero tenet rem mensurandum, quasi retrahat
a mensura, vel pondere. reponitur in loco.
Fit vero cum Luna decurrit sub stellis quae Virginis
palmam figurant sinistrae manus in qua Spica tenet,
et hora sus cum stellis horoscopat. Dicat artifex,
Nichil prorsus in hac apotheca vendatur, vel in
hoc loco mensuretur, aut ponderetur.
IMAGO quae proiecta in aquam fontis, aut

it is to be cast into the river or lake.

THE METHOD OF AN IMAGE to prevent a field from being cultivated:

The image of a broken ploughshare shall be fashioned when the Moon,
in its hour, rises with the stars which appear above the head of Virgo. The artificer shall say,
no plough shall penetrate this soil, and any set against it
shall be broken. The image is to be buried in the four corners of the field.

AN IMAGE so that, when it is deposited in a place where
things are sold, or in a warehouse,
(those goods) shall not be sold, either by weight or by quantity: An image shall be fashioned
of a man in whose left hand is a balance, or a sextarius[110] (vessel),
but in the right he holds a thing to be measured, as though withholding it
from being measured or weighed. The image is to be deposited in the place (intended).
But is shall be (fashioned) when the Moon, in its hour, rises with the stars which
comprise the palm of Virgo's left hand, in which she grasps Spica. The artificer shall say,
nothing at all shall be sold in this warehouse, or
measured or weighed in this place.

AN IMAGE which, cast into the water of a spring or

---

110 A Roman unit of volume, slightly less than 26 modern liters.

putei scaturientis, sistit aquas, et exsiccari prorsus
facit. figuratur hominis imago tenentis vas aquae
plenum quam ex fonte exaurit, et not effundit.
proiiciatur in fontem, aut puteum. Dicat artifex,
Exauriantur aquae omnes ex hoc puteo aut fonte,
et non exscaturiant ultra. fit vero quotiens Luna
decurrit sub stellis caudae ursae minoris, et
caudae Capricorni, et cum illis horoscopat hora sua.
MODUS IMAGINIS cuius praesentia ligantur omnia
instrumenta, et destruuntur, et rumpuntur. figuratur
imago sonantis tibiam, et hoc quotiens ☽ decurrit
sub stellis quae figurantur in dextra palma manus
retinentis habenas, et cum hiis horoscopat hora sua.
Dicat artifex, Dissonus fiat omne instrumentum
ad huius imaginis praesentiam, et praesentet, aut
tangat instrumentum musicum.
IMAGO eiusdem posse cuius est figura vir
sonans fistulam. fit vero haec quotiens Luna decurrens
sub stellis capitis Geminorum horoscopat cum illis

flowing cistern, halts the waters, and causes them to dry up completely:
An image shall be fashioned of a person holding a vessel full of water which has been drawn from a spring, and the spring is not flowing. The image is to be cast into a spring or cistern. The artificer shall say, *all the waters of this cistern or spring shall be exhausted, and flow no more.* But the image shall be (fashioned) when the Moon, in its hour, rises with the stars comprising the tails of both the Little Bear and Capricorn.

THE METHOD OF AN IMAGE by the presence of which all instruments may be bound, and destroyed, and broken:
An image shall be fashioned of a piping flute, and this (is done) when the Moon, in its hour, rises with the stars which appear in the palm of the right hand holding the reins.[111]
The artificer shall say, *every instrument shall become dissonant in the presence of this image*, and it is to be presented or touched to the musical instrument.

AN IMAGE having the same power is the figure of a man playing a pipe, but this shall be (fashioned) when the Moon, in its hour, rises with the stars of the heads of Gemini.

---

[111] Presumably referring to Auriga.

hora sua. Dicat artifex, Dissonus fiat, et
stupidus omne instrumentum musicum ad
huius imaginis praesentiam.
IMAGINIS MODUS quae loco sepulta
facit ut vermes corrodat terrae nascentium
radices, et quaecumque corrodi apta sunt. figuratur
imago vermis unius, aut plurium involutorum
radicibus, et herbis. fit autem cum decurrit Luna
sub stellis signatis in cauda leporis, et supra
os canis anterioris, et super remo navis, et
hora sua cum hiis horoscopat. Dicat artifex,
Corrodant vermes radices omnes, et herbas, et
terrae nascentia agri huius. et sepeliatur in
quatuor angulus agri.
IMAGINIS MODUS cuius praesentia non iacit
arcus, aut balista, aut rumpitur ad huius praesentiam.
figuratur homo extendens arcum quasi
iaciens, et frangitur. fit autem quotiens ☾ decurrit
sub stellis quae figurantur supra collum maioris

GIORGIO ANSELMI / Brian Johnson

[36r]

The artificer shall say,
every instrument shall become dissonant and dull in
the presence of this image.
THE METHOD OF AN IMAGE which, buried in a place,
makes it so that worms shall gnaw the
roots growing in the soil, and whatsoever is fit to be gnawed:
An image is fashioned of one or more worms winding around
roots and herbs. And this shall be done when the Moon, in its hour, rises with
the stars appearing in the tail of the Hare, and above
the mouth of the Little Dog, and above the oar of the Ship.
The artificer shall say,
worms shall gnaw all the roots, and herbs, and
new growth of this farmland. And the image is to be buried in
the four corners of a field.
THE METHOD OF AN IMAGE in the presence of which
a bow or ballista will not shoot, or otherwise will break:
(An image) is fashioned of a person holding forth a bow as though
to shoot, and the bow breaking. And this is done when the Moon, in its hour, rises with
the stars which appear above the neck of the Great

ursae, et caput ♌, et hora sua cum illis horoscopat.
Dicat artifex, Non iaciat arcus, neque balista,
aut rumpatur ad huius praesentiam.
IMAGINIS MODUS mirabilis movens
homines qui supra eam transeunt, ad iram, et supra
eam firmantur. figura est stantis hominis, et irati.
fit autem quotiens ☽ decurrit sub stellis quae pinguntur
super dimidium mulieris quae non novit virum,
et horoscopat cum illis hora sua. Sepeliatur
in loco transitus. Dicat artifex, Non transeat
homo, quin stet, et irascatur.
IMAGINIS MODUS ad cuius praesentiam cla-
mitant homines, et manus erigunt. figuratur
hominis imago qualis clamantis, et manus eri-
gentis. fit vero quotiens decurrit ☽ sub stellis
minoris ursae, et dimidio navis, et navis
initio, et cum hiis horoscopat. sepeliatur in loco
transitus. Dicat artifex, Quicumque super locum
hunc transit, clamet, et manus erigat.

Giorgio Anselmi / Brian Johnson

Bear, and the head of Leo.
The artificer shall say, *neither bow nor ballista shall fire, or otherwise shall break, in the presence of this image.*
THE METHOD OF AN IMAGE marvelous for inciting to anger those people who pass over it, and
making them recalcitrant: The figure is of a person standing, and angry.
And this is (fashioned) when the Moon, in its hour, rises with the stars which appear
over the middle of "the woman who has not known a man".[112]
It is to be buried
in a place through which people pass. The artificer shall say, *no person shall pass without stopping and becoming angry.*
THE METHOD OF AN IMAGE in the presence of which
people will cry out and raise their hands: An image is fashioned
of a person who appears to be crying out and raising their hands.
But this is done when the Moon rises with the stars
of the Little Bear, and aligns with the middle of the Ship, and
the first part thereof. The image is to be buried in a place
through which people pass. The artificer shall say, *whosoever passes over this place shall cry out and raise their hands.*

---

[112] Presumably Virgo, though the same phrase is used earlier in the text to identify Andromeda.

Divinum Opus de Magia Disciplina

IMAGINIS MODUS cuius praesentia cantant
homines. et est figuretur imago hominis sedentis
super sua stramina, percutientis cytharam, et
cantantis eum ea. et hoc cum ☽ decurrit
sub stellis dimidii Virginis, et quae in eius
sinistra palma ponuntur. Dicat artifex,
Cantent viri et mulieres quotiens super hunc locum
transeunt. Sepelitur sub loco transitus.
IMAGINIS MODUS cuius praesentia, reponunt
homines vestimenta sua in terra, et recumbant
super ea. figuratur imago viri nudi, recum-
bentis super vestimenta sua, et tenentis sinistram
manum super caput suus, dextram vero elevet
in coelum. fit autem quotiens decurrit ☽ sub stellis quae
pinguntur super brachium Virginis, et eius genu
dextro; et cum hiis horoscopat hora sua. Dicat
artifex, Quicumque super hunc locum transierit,
vestimenta deponat, et super ea nudus
recumbat.

GIORGIO ANSELMI / Brian Johnson

[37r]

THE METHOD OF AN IMAGE in the presence of which
people will sing: And the image is fashioned like a person sitting
upon their bed, plucking a cythara, and
singing along with it. And this is done when the Moon travels
under the stars in the middle of Virgo, and which
are placed in her left palm. The artificer shall say,
men and women shall sing when they pass over this place.
The image is to be buried under a place through which they travel.
THE METHOD OF AN IMAGE in the presence of which
people will place their clothes on the ground and lie
upon them: An image is fashioned of a naked man lying
upon his clothes, and holding his left
hand over his head, but raising his right
toward the sky. And this is done when the Moon, in its hour, rises
  with the stars which
appear over the right arm and knee of Virgo.
The artificer shall say, *whosoever passes over this place
shall put off their clothes and lie naked upon them.*

Divinum Opus de Magia Disciplina

IMAGO AD IDEM. figuratur imago viri
nudi, quotiens decurrit ☽ sub stellis borealis co-
rone, et coronae Scorpionis, et hora sua
cum illis horoscopat.
IMAGINIS MODUS cuius praesentia mu-
lieres cantant, et caput suum pectunt, et scalpunt.
figuratur imago sedentis mulieris, ore clausos
pectantis caput pectine. fit quotiens decurrit
Luna sub stellis quae figurant caput Algol,
et caput Persei: et cum illis horoscopat hora
sua. Dicat artifex, Non transeat mulier
super hanc imaginem quin pectinet, aut
scalpat caput suum.
IMAGINIS MODUS, quae in domo, aut hos-
pitio reposita facit ut habitantes non cessent
comedere, neque saturari valeant. figuretur
hominis imago voraciter comedentis. et hoc
quotiens decurrit ☽ cum stellis quae positae sunt
super genua et crura et pedes Persei, et cum eis

AN IMAGE FOR THE SAME: An image of
a naked man is fashioned when the Moon, in its hour, rises with the stars of the Northern
Crown and the Crown of the Scorpion.[113]
THE METHOD OF AN IMAGE in the presence of which women
will sing, and comb and scratch their heads:
An image is fashioned of a woman sitting, mouth closed,
combing her head with a comb. This is done when
the Moon, in its hour, rises with the stars which comprise Caput Algol
and the head of Perseus.
The artificer shall say, *no woman shall pass
over this image without combing or
scratching her head.*
THE METHOD OF AN IMAGE which, placed in a house or
inn, makes it so that the inhabitants shall not stop
eating, nor can they be satisfied: An image is fashioned
of a person eating voraciously, and this is done
when the Moon, in its hour, rises with the stars which are set
upon the knees, and legs, and feet of Perseus.

---

113 The Crown of the Scorpion comprises the three stars Acrab (from the Arabic for "scorpion"; β Scorpii), Jabha (Arabic for "forehead"; δ Scorpii), and Fang (from the Chinese for "room"; π Scorpii, itself actually a triple star).

Divinum Opus de Magia Disciplina

[38r]

horoscopat hora sua. Dicat artifex, Dum sepelitur
eam in loco, non saturetur homo come-
dens in hoc loco, neque cesset comedere.
IMAGINIS MODUS cuius praesentia cantant
mulieres. figurantur imago mulieris
cantantis fistula. et hoc quotiens decurrit
Luna sub stellis cadentis vulturis, et
eius caudae summitate. Canat, et plaudat
mulier quaecumque super hunc locum transierit.
Sepeliatur autem in loco transitus.
IMAGO MODUS cuius praesentia mulier
saepius it, et reddit super eodem loco. figuretur
imago puellae quasi euntis. fit autem cum Luna
decurrit sub stellis maioris ursae, et cum illis
horoscopat hora sua. Dicat artifex, Mulier
quaecumque super hac imagine transierit, eat, redeat
frequens. Sepelitur in loco transitus.

EXPLICIT TRACTATUS 4.^{s} DE IMAGINIBUS
MAGISTRI GEORGII PARMENSIS.
1542. DIE. FEBRUARII.

GIORGIO ANSELMI / Brian Johnson

[38r]

The artificer shall say, *while this image is buried*
in a place, no person eating
in that place shall be satisfied, nor cease eating.
THE METHOD OF AN IMAGE in the presence of which
women will sing: An image is fashioned of a woman
singing along to a pipe, and this is done when
the Moon travels under the stars of the Falling Vulture, and
the uppermost part of its tail.
Any woman who passes over this place shall sing and clap,
so long as the image is buried in a place though which women travel.
THE METHOD OF AN IMAGE in the presence of which a woman
will go and return to the same place repeatedly: An image is
    fashioned
of a girl who appears to be going somewhere, and this is done when
    the Moon,
in its hour, rises with the stars of the Great Bear.
The artificer shall say,
any woman passing over this image shall go and return
again and again. It is to be buried in a place through which women
    travel.

THE END OF THE FOURTH TRACTATE: ON IMAGES
BY MASTER GEORGE OF PARMA
1542, THE [...] DAY OF FEBRUARY.

Bibliography

MANUSCRIPTS

Florence, Biblioteca Medicea Laurenziana, MS Plut. 44.35
Vatican City, Biblioteca Apostolica Vaticana, MS Vat. lat. 4080
——————, MS Vat. lat. 5333

OTHER PRIMARY SOURCES

Agrippa, Heinrich Cornelius. *Three Books of Occult Philosophy*. Eric Purdue, trans. Inner Traditions (2021).
Albertus Magnus. *Book of Minerals*. Dorothy Wyckoff, trans. Clarendon Press (1967).
——————. *Speculum Astronomiae*. Charles S. F. Burnett et al., trans. In Paola Zambelli, *The* Speculum Astronomiae *and Its Enigma: Astrology, Theology and Science in Albertus Magnus and his Contemporaries* (Springer, 1992), pp. 202–73.
al-Kindi, Abu Yusuf Ya'qub ibn Ishaq. *De Radiis*. Scott Gosnell, trans. Black Letter Press (2022).
Aristotle. *Metaphysics, Books X–XIV; Oeconomica; Magna Moralia*. Hugh Tredennick and G. Cyril Armstrong, trans. Harvard University Press (1935).
——————. *On the Heavens*. W. K. C. Guthrie, trans. Harvard University Press (1939).
——————. *Physics, Books I–IV*. Philip H. Wicksteed and Francis M. Cornford, trans. Harvard University Press (1929).
——————. *Posterior Analytics; Topica*. Hugh Tredennick and Edward S. Forster, trans. Harvard University Press (1960).
Attrell, Dan and David Porreca (trans.) 2019. *Picatrix: A Medieval Treatise on Astral Magic*. Pennsylvania State University Press.
Bohak, Gideon and Charles Burnett (eds., trans.) 2021. *Thabit ibn Qurra* On Talismans *and Ps.-Ptolemy* On Images *1–9 together with the* Liber prestigiorum Thebidis *of Adelard of Bath*. SISMEL, Edizioni del Galluzzo.
Carmody, Francis J. (ed.) 1960. *The Astronomical Works of Thabit b. Qurra*. University of California Press.
Copenhaver, Brian P. (trans.) 1992. *Hermetica*. Cambridge University Press.
Houlding, Deborah (ed.) 2006. Ptolemy's Centiloquium. Henry Coley, trans. https://www.skyscript.co.uk/centiloquium1.html. Accessed 11 November, 2023.

BIBLIOGRAPHY

Leonardi, Camillo. *The Mirror of Stones:* Speculum Lapidum, *Book III: An Astrological Lapidary*. Margherita Fiorello, trans. Revelore Press (2022).
Litwa, M. David (trans.) 2018. *Hermetica II*. Cambridge University Press.
Macrobius. *Commentary on the Dream of Scipio*. William Harris Stahl, trans. Columbia University Press (1952).
Plato. *Timaeus*. Donald J. Zeyl, trans. In John M. Cooper, ed., *Plato: Complete Works* (Hackett, 1997), pp. 1224–91.
Ptolemy. *Tetrabiblos*. F.E. Robbins, trans. Harvard University Press (1940).
Shumaker, Wayne (ed., trans.) 1978. *John Dee on Astronomy:* Propaedeumata Aphoristica *(1558 and 1568), Latin and English*. University of California Press.

SECONDARY LITERATURE

Bezza, Giuseppe. 2015. Saturn–Jupiter Conjunctions and General Astrology: Ptolemy, Abū Maʿshar and Their Commentators. In Charles Burnett and Dorian Gieseler Greenbaum, eds., *From Māshā'allāh to Kepler: Theory and Practice in Medieval and Renaissance Astrology* (Sophia Centre Press), pp. 5–48.
Burnett, Charles. 1996. The Scapulimancy of Giorgio Anselmi's *Divinum opus de magia disciplina*. In Charles Burnett, ed., *Magic and Divination in the Middle Ages: Texts and Techniques in the Islamic and Christian Worlds* (Routledge), pp. 63–81.
———. 1992. The Translating Activity in Medieval Spain. In Salma Khadra Jayyusi, ed., *The Legacy of Muslim Spain* (Brill), pp. 1036–58.
Cox, Merlin. 2005. *Similar Stars and Strange Angels: Giorgio Anselmi's Astrological Magic*. Master's thesis, University of London.
de Vore, Nicholas. 2002 [1947]. *Encyclopedia of Astrology*. Astrology Classics Publishing.
Hafez, Ihsan. 2010. *Abd al-Rahman al-Sufi and His Book of the Fixed Stars: A Journey of Re-discovery*. PhD thesis, James Cook University.
Juste, David. 2023. Pseudo-Ptolemy, *De imaginibus super facies signorum*. http://ptolemaeus.badw.de/work/4. Accessed 11 November, 2023.
———. 2023b. Pseudo-Ptolemy, *Liber de impressionibus imaginum, anulorum et sigillorum secundum facies duodecim signorum zodiaci*. https://ptolemaeus.badw.de/work/64. Accessed 22 December, 2023.
Klaassen, Frank. 2013. *The Transformations of Magic: Illicit Learned Magic in the Later Middle Ages and Renaissance*. Pennsylvania State University Press.
Kunitzsch, Paul. 1987. Peter Apian and 'Azophi': Arabic Constellations in Renaissance Astronomy. *Journal for the History of Astronomy* 18 (2): 117–24.
Lewis, James R. 2003. *The Astrology Book*. Visible Ink Press (second edition).

BIBLIOGRAPHY

Mayor, Adrienne. 2010. *The Poison King: The Life and Legend of Mithradates, Rome's Deadliest Enemy*. Princeton University Press.

Page, Sophie. 2019. A Late Medieval Demonic Invasion of the Heavens. In David J. Collins, ed., *The Sacred and the Sinister: Studies in Medieval Religion and Magic* (Pennsylvania State University Press), pp. 233–54.

Rubin, Jonathan. 2014. The Use of the 'Jericho Tyrus' in Theriac: A Case Study in the History of the Exchanges of Medical Knowledge Between Western Europe and the Realm of Islam in the Middle Ages. *Medium Aevum* 83: 234–53.

Thorndike, Lynn. 1934. *History of Magic and Experimental Science*, volume IV. Columbia University Press.

Tomlinson, Gary. 1993. *Music in Renaissance Magic: Toward a Historiography of Others*. University of Chicago Press.

Walker, D. P. 2000 [1958]. *Spiritual and Demonic Magic: From Ficino to Campanella*. Pennsylvania State University Press.

Weill-Parot, Nicholas (in collaboration with Julien Véronèse). 2012. Antonio da Montolmo's *De occultis et manifestis* or *Liber intelligentiarum*: An Annotated Critical Edition with English Translation and Introduction. In Claire Fanger, ed., *Invoking Angels: Theurgic Ideas and Practices, Thirteenth to Sixteenth Centuries* (Pennsylvania State University Press), pp. 219–93.

Weill-Parot, Nicholas. 2019. Jerome Torrella and "Astrological Images". In Sophie Page and Catherine Rider, eds., *The Routledge History of Medieval Magic* (Routledge), pp. 254–67.

Wolfson, Harry A. 1962. The Problem of the Souls of the Spheres from the Byzantine Commentaries on Aristotle Through the Arabs and St. Thomas to Kepler. *Dumbarton Oaks Papers* 16: 65–93.

Zambelli, Paola. 1992. *The Speculum Astronomiae and Its Enigma: Astrology, Theology and Science in Albertus Magnus and his Contemporaries*. Springer.

Zieme, Stefan. 2023. Gerard of Cremona's Latin Translation of the *Almagest* and the Revision of Tables. *Journal for the History of Astronomy* 54 (1): 3–33.

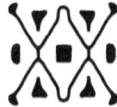

A Similitude of Nature was typeset by Joseph Uccello in the Spring of 2025, using Rosart, Hercules, Epicene, Ogg, Ready, Alverata, and Akkurat.

www.ingramcontent.com/pod-product-compliance
Lightning Source LLC
Chambersburg PA
CBHW030534080526
44586CB00011B/439